Things They Didn't Tell Me
30 Lessons Learned as a New Pastor

WREN HUDSON

WH Creations Publishing

Southaven, Mississippi

Copyright © 2025 by Wren Hudson.

All rights reserved. No part of this publication may be reproduced, stored in a retrieval system, or transmitted in any form or by any means, electronic, mechanical, photocopying, recording, or otherwise, without the publisher's prior written permission.

Scripture quotations are taken from the Holy Bible, New International Version (NIV).
Used by permission. All rights reserved worldwide.

Printed in the United States of America.

ISBN: 979-8-218-82059-6

Published by WH Creations Publishing
Edited by Peace Onwuka

To my wife, Nerry, and our daughter, Neriyah — my greatest gifts and daily reminders of God's faithfulness.

And to all pastors beginning ministry, may these lessons bring hope and peace.

Acknowledgments

I sincerely thank Nerry, my wife, for her love, patience, and partnership during my ministry. To Neriyah, our daughter: her laughter shows me daily that joy is sacred.

To my family, who have always believed in my calling, and to the members I've been privileged to pastor, thank you for teaching me what real ministry looks like.

To my mentors and colleagues in ministry, thank you for your counsel, prayers, and honest conversations about what it means to lead with integrity.

To the critics, who tested my faith and patience, you taught me grace and perseverance.

This book is here because of all the support I received.

FOREWORD

When my pastoral ministry began almost 20 years ago, I was thrust into two churches that had seen their fair share of ups and downs. It was honestly like being thrown into a lake and told to swim. There were so many personalities, undercurrents of confusion, and dramas being played out, and the expectation was that, as the pastor, it was my job to try to solve all these problems through the power of God.

Having gone to the seminary, I had learned a lot of book knowledge, but nothing can really prepare you for the experience of pastoring a church until you're thrown into the fire. No book can really teach you how to deal with fanatics who want to take over your church. No book can really prepare you for the conservatives who threaten to leave the church if you initiate even the slightest changes to the worship service. No book can really prepare you for a board meeting where your elder makes threats towards you, or a woman tries to come onto you, or a fatherless child latches hold to you, or your spouse threatens to leave you, or your family feels neglected by you, or your pastoral boss plans to move you just when you're getting ready to do something in the district. No book can truly prepare you for ministry; only Jesus can.

Nevertheless, in this book, Pastor Hudson sheds pertinent insights on what it's like to be a new pastor. Through his own experience in ministry, he provides valuable lessons for other pastors preparing to start their ministry journey. Sensing the need for new pastors to be more prepared as they're plunged into church life, Pastor Hudson shares his burden in this raw, riveting, and rational treatise.

A recent Barna study revealed that 42% of pastors considered quitting the ministry, and as a pastor myself, I can understand why. The never-ending stress of ministering to the sick, dealing with the divisive, loving the unlovable, and sharing in the cares and burdens of broken people takes its toll on the best men. However, Pastor Hudson's book is meant to give pastors renewed hope that they can make it despite the obstacles involved in ministry. It is not true that you won't work a day if you do what you like. Ministry is HARD work even for those who were truly called! Yet with God on your side, He can make something beautiful of your ministry.

I've had the privilege of knowing Pastor Wren Hudson for about 3-4 years. I remember when he first visited our church in Pensacola, FL, with one of his colleagues. He was not engaged in official ministry then, but you could sense the call upon his life. Energetic, visionary, and possessed of a strong desire to do all he could for the cause of Christ, he quickly plunged himself into the mission and ministry of our local church in the Pensacola area. His impact can still be felt in preaching, singing, and working with the audio-visual ministry.

He went on to live in the New York City area, where he met and married his lovely wife while still working for God in the local churches, and I remember so plainly as we met again while I was up there preaching for another friend. Nevertheless, God had even bigger plans for him, as he got a call to full-time ministry in Mississippi, and in just a little over a year and a half, we've seen his district add numerous souls to the kingdom. It has been a great honor and blessing for me

Foreword

to have gotten to know this mighty man of God and his lovely wife, Nerry, who stands shoulder to shoulder with him in the work of the Lord.

From personal experience, I know that Pastor Hudson is a scholarly, professional, and dedicated young man who loves God and the work of God. During our conversations, I have been impressed by his depth and hunger to learn and grow. This depth bleeds over into his writing, and you will definitely come away from this treatise wanting even more.

I pray that this book will speak to the hearts of young and old ministers. To the seasoned minister, I pray that this book encourages you to keep pushing toward the finish line and leave a legacy of unwavering dedication to the cause of Christ to the very end. While for the younger minister, I pray that this book encourages you to keep running your ministry race, knowing that while it might seem long, a great reward awaits you. As the author of Hebrews said in Hebrews 12:1-2,

> "Wherefore seeing we also are compassed about with so great a cloud of witnesses, let us lay aside every weight, and the sin which doth so easily beset us, and let us run with patience the race that is set before us, Looking unto Jesus the author and finisher of our faith; who for the joy that was set before him endured the cross, despising the shame, and is set down at the right hand of the throne of God."

— Dr. Dejuan Knight, *Mentor & Senior Pastor, Hillview Seventh-day Adventist Church*

INTRODUCTION

When I first accepted the call to pastoral ministry, I carried a heart full of zeal, a Bible in my hand, and a head full of dreams. I believed that preparation from school, mentors, and books would be enough. I thought I knew what I was stepping into. However, I discovered that there are things no classroom, no professor, and no orientation session can ever prepare you for.

This book, *Things They Didn't Tell Me: 30 Lessons Learned as a New Pastor*, was born out of my own baptism by fire into the ministry. These pages are not theories. They are scars, stories, mistakes, mercies, struggles, and small victories. Each lesson is written not as a complaint but as a testimony of God's sustaining grace.

If you are a new pastor, I want you to know this: the journey is beautiful and brutal. Ministry is holy work, but it will stretch you in ways you never imagined. You will be confronted with expectations you never agreed to, conflicts you never saw coming, and responsibilities you were never trained for. And yet, you will also witness the presence of God in ways you never dreamed possible.

These lessons are not meant to overwhelm you with warnings, but to anchor you in reality. They are here to give you perspective when the ground beneath you shatters. Think of them as signposts; reminders that you are not the first to walk this road and will not be the last. Every generation of pastors learns its own hard lessons. The difference is whether you choose to let those lessons make you bitter or let them make you better.

I pray that as you read, you will see yourself somewhere in these pages. You may find reassurance that your struggles are not unique. You may discover strategies to help you navigate seasons of fatigue, criticism, or loneliness. Most of all, I hope you find encouragement that even in the most challenging ministry moments, God remains faithful and continues to form you. "He who calls you is faithful; He will surely do it" (1 Thessalonians 5:24).

This book is not long by design. You can carry it in your bag, flip to a lesson when you need perspective, or reread it during a dry season. Each chapter is brief but weighty, pointing you back to Christ, the only One who can carry both you and the people you serve.

Pastoring will break you, but God will use it to remake you. In that remaking, you will discover that the most significant lesson is not how to pastor God's people but how to let God pastor you.

Welcome to the journey!

CONTENTS

Pastoring Feels Like Work, Even When You Love It **1**

Learning Finance on the Job **5**

You Cannot Change People—Only God Can **11**

Balance Begins with Boundaries **17**

Understanding Different Types of Critics **23**

Many Leaders Wrestle with Their Own Conversion **29**

You Will Face Dry Seasons **37**

Prioritizing Preparation for Worship Leadership **43**

Pastoring is Not the Same as Your Walk **49**

God Uses Ministry to Save Pastors Too **57**

Rest is Essential **65**

Making Hard Decisions is Unavoidable **73**

Always Have Multiple Plans for Logistics **77**

Most Members Will Not Be Interested in Evangelism **83**

Pastoring by God's Direction **89**

Youth Are Vulnerable and Require Authenticity **97**

Adjusting to Different Cultures in Ministry **103**

Some People Love Conflict and Do Not Desire Peace **109**

Dealing with Gossip **115**

Extending Grace When People Lack Integrity **121**

Some People are Untrainable **129**

Struggling with Comparison **135**

Wait on God's Timing **141**

Loneliness in Ministry **147**

Cultivating Life Outside of Ministry **151**

Protecting Your Marriage in Ministry **157**

The Trust Test **165**

Pastor Your Community **173**

Your Vision Is Limited; Rely on the Holy Spirit **179**

If Anything Else Brings You Joy, Do That **185**

The Journey Continues **189**

PART I – WHEN REALITY HITS

CHAPTER 1

Pastoring Feels Like Work, Even When You Love It

I was prepared when I stepped into my first pastoral assignment, or so I thought. Having studied theology, completed various trainings, and served alongside experienced pastors, I believed I was ready to lead on my own. Yet nothing truly prepares you for the moment you realize it is all on you. My wife and I packed our lives in the Northeast and moved to Mississippi. We had no children yet, but we trusted God's leading into a strange and unfamiliar place.

Everything was new: a new state, a new culture, and a new way of life. Coming from a Caribbean background, the Deep South felt foreign in almost every way. The pace was slower, the traditions were different, and the unspoken expectations of Southern church life were unlike anything I had known. My wife had just left her job to follow me into ministry. We had no family nearby, no built-in support system, and no safety net. We had also been married for only six months. It was our season to lean on God and on each other. Some days that felt like enough. Other days, it did not.

My first assignment included four small churches in tiny towns. On paper, that sounded manageable, even exciting, as though it were an opportunity to do something meaningful.

In Jamaica, where I grew up, pastors often led multiple congregations, and this approach worked because strong lay leadership carried much of the load. But this was not Jamaica. In Mississippi, congregations relied on their pastors for everything. Four churches meant four distinct cultures, four sets of expectations, four different visions of what their pastor should be, and one person trying to hold it all together.

Three days after my installation, reality struck. One of my churches was about to have its electricity turned off. The funds in their account were almost gone, and the bill was overdue. I did not have $400 to spare, and even if I did, should I give it? Would that be enabling poor stewardship, or was this my moment to be the hands and feet of Christ? These were questions my training never addressed.

That became my first crisis as a pastor. It was not a theological debate or a stirring sermon. It was not even a difficult board meeting. It was simply a matter of figuring out how to keep the lights on. The congregation had only a few elderly members and had been declining for years. Their situation made sense: an aging population, a shrinking community, and decades of slow decline. I understood, but understanding did not make it less overwhelming for someone three days into ministry.

In that moment, one truth became clear. People often say, "If you do what you love, you will never work a day in your life." That is not true in pastoral ministry. You can love this calling with all your heart and still find it an exhausting and demanding job. It will keep you up at night and test your marriage, your faith, and your sense of calling. Love does not erase labor. Yet love keeps you laboring when the work feels heavier than you ever imagined. Sometimes, love is the only thing that does.

The Lesson

Pastoring is not effortless. It demands long hours, hard decisions, emotional resilience, and constant adjustment. Loving the work does not make it any less work, but it gives you the strength to continue when everything in you wants to quit. Ministry stretches you precisely because it is holy work. It calls you to carry the burdens of people, systems, and communities larger than yourself.

A Biblical Reflection

I think of Moses in Exodus 3 when God called him to deliver Israel. Moses immediately pointed out his limitations and asked, "Who am I that I should go to Pharaoh?" (Exodus 3:11). God's reply was simple: "I will be with you." The same assurance holds true for us as pastors. You will encounter responsibilities the seminary never mentioned and face problems no manual has ever described, such as unpaid electric bills just three days into your first assignment. But remember this: you did not call yourself; God did. And if God calls you, He will equip you, even in the face of overwhelming hardship.

Encouragement for New Pastors

If you are starting, expect the unexpected. Your first challenge may not come from the pulpit. It might be unpaid bills, broken HVAC systems, outdated technology, or church members who have not spoken to each other in years. Do not be discouraged when the reality of ministry feels heavier than what your passion can carry. Remember that the weight of the work is meant to draw you closer to God, not push you away.

You will love this calling, but that love will not make it easier. It will, however, sustain your perseverance when ministry feels less like a dream and more like labor. And when the labor wears you down, remember that the God who called you is the same God who equips you. Ministry will demand much from you, more than you think you have to give, but God's presence will always provide more. Always!

CHAPTER 2

Learning Finance on the Job

One of the first pieces of advice I received as a new pastor was both daunting and direct: "Review the finances of your churches." At the time, I had no idea how important those words were or what they even meant. My ministerial training had prepared me in theology, Greek, Hebrew, homiletics, and hermeneutics, but it had not covered topics such as budgets, audits, or balance sheets. I assumed financial management belonged solely to the treasurer. That assumption did not last long. While the treasurer records and reports, the pastor is ultimately the senior custodian of the church. Every department, financial decision, and dollar, whether spent or unspent, rests under your oversight, whether you feel ready for it or not.

This realization pushed me into unfamiliar territory. I had four congregations, each with its own financial story. Some had not completed a proper audit in years. Others had records so incomplete that an audit was impossible. During my orientation, the treasurer handed me four brown envelopes, each containing a statement of debt owed to the conference. I remember staring at those envelopes, feeling the weight of numbers I could not yet interpret. One congregation had fewer than five members, only one of whom earned a steady income, yet the church owed nearly $20,000. How could such a small group carry such a burden? How was I supposed to lead them through it? Selling the building briefly crossed my mind. It all felt impossible.

So what does it mean to "review the finances"? It means carefully studying several key areas.

Remittances: Examine tithes and local offerings, not just for one year but over several years, to identify giving patterns. Are people giving consistently? Are there seasonal changes? What trends stand out?

Cash Flow: Review checking accounts, savings, and investments to understand available resources. Do not stop at the balance sheet. Know what funds are restricted or designated for specific purposes.

Debts and Overheads: Identify what the church owes and what recurring costs drain its income. Some obligations are obvious; others are hidden in forgotten loan agreements or deferred maintenance.

One consistent pattern quickly emerged. While tithe giving remained strong, offerings often lagged. This matters deeply. The tithe supports the global mission of the church, but offerings sustain the local congregation. Offerings keep the lights on, maintain the building, and fund local ministries. When offerings decline, the local church weakens.

Over time, I learned that financial statements tell stories if you learn to read them. Numbers reveal seasons of health and decline, moments of unity and conflict, and even the pulse of the church's spiritual life. Financial fluctuations often mirrored the church's emotional and spiritual climate. A new pastoral assignment, internal conflict, or community crisis left visible traces in the records. Understanding those patterns helped me discern where stewardship teaching was needed through sermons, workshops, or personal conversations.

At first, I felt lost. Then I discovered a truth that applies far beyond finances: it is okay not to know, as long as you are willing to learn. Ignorance becomes dangerous only when it is paired with pride. Pretending to understand would have set me up for failure. Instead, I asked for help. I sought out experienced pastors, patient treasurers, and wise conference officers who explained the basics and guided me through financial reports. I asked questions that sounded simple. I admitted confusion when I felt it. Books and tutorials were helpful, but the most valuable lessons came from conversations with those who had already walked this road.

The Lesson

Church finances are not optional knowledge for pastors. You don't need to be an accountant, but you do need to understand the basics. Financial ignorance doesn't protect you. It exposes you. A financially healthy church is not necessarily one with large reserves. It's one with consistent giving, steady systems for handling money, and the ability to meet obligations without constantly living in crisis mode. If a pastor ignores finances, they and the church can be undone by neglect. I've seen it happen. Good pastors, faithful preachers, were brought down not by scandal but by financial mismanagement that they didn't even know was happening.

A Biblical Reflection

Stewardship is central to Scripture. Malachi 3 calls God's people to faithfulness in returning tithes and offerings. Jesus Himself taught, "Give, and it will be given to you; a good measure, pressed down, shaken together, and running over" (Luke 6:38). Faithful giving is not just about money; it is about obedience, trust, and partnership with God's mission. As a pastor, understanding the financial condition of your church enables you to lead people into deeper faithfulness. Why? Because stewardship is, in fact, discipleship. How people handle money reveals what they truly believe about God.

Encouragement for New Pastors

If you are new to ministry, take this to heart: do not neglect financial literacy. I know it feels overwhelming. I know you didn't go into the ministry to read spreadsheets, but this matters. Take a course if you can. Many denominations offer them. Watch YouTube tutorials on reading financial statements. Ask your conference treasurer to sit down with you and explain a remittance report line by line. Don't just glance at it during board meetings. Learn how to read it. Study a financial statement until you understand the basics of cash flow, expenses, and debt. You may love preaching, visiting, or teaching, but your ministry will suffer if you cannot steward your church's finances.

It will feel like work because it is. It will stretch you beyond what you thought ministry required. However, as you grow in this area, you will discover that financial health is not just about numbers but about freeing your congregation to focus on its mission rather than mere survival. And that is one of the most pastoral things you can do. Because a church drowning in debt can't focus on mission. Financial health creates space for spiritual health.

CHAPTER 3

You Cannot Change People - Only God Can

At the beginning of my ministry, I believed I could fix everything. I saw inefficiencies in worship, gaps in communication, weak accountability, and a need for renewed energy in evangelism. I noticed a great deal of potential, but just as many obstacles standing in the way. My instinct was to move quickly, implement systems, and reorganize everything so the church could operate more efficiently. My intentions were good. I wanted to see the church grow and bring glory to God. My motives were pure, but my timing was poor. I underestimated how deeply people were attached to the existing systems. What I saw as outdated structures were, for them, sacred traditions, memories, and markers of identity that shaped their experience of church for generations.

Change without trust is not real change. At best, it produces compliance. People may allow you to implement new systems, but once you move on, they quietly return to what they know. I have watched this cycle repeat many times. What I once thought was progress turned out to be temporary motion. I was working hard, but I was working alone. And that is exhausting.

During that season, I learned how people genuinely respond to change. Some do not want it. The current system, even when flawed, feels safe and predictable. They understand it, they know their place in it, and change feels threatening. Many would rather live with a dysfunction they can manage than face a transformation they cannot control. Others are not opposed to change, but they want to observe before committing. They need to see that your leadership is trustworthy, your vision is grounded in Scripture, and your strategy has substance. These are your early adopters. If you gain their trust, they become strong partners. If you lose it, you lose them entirely. Some are open to change but need time to process it. They become your best allies when given the freedom to move at their own pace. My eagerness to move too quickly created more resistance than results. I confused motion with progress and speed with effectiveness. Both were mistakes.

Eventually, I realized that my task was not to force change but to facilitate it. I am not the change agent. The Holy Spirit is. My responsibility is to create space for Him to work. My job is not to transform hearts but to make room for God to do so. That means praying, listening, discerning, and presenting God's vision clearly, then stepping back. I can organize and strategize, but no plan will last unless God Himself moves the hearts of His people.

The Lesson

Change in the church must be Spirit-driven, not pastor-driven. Your ideas are not automatically God's, no matter how good and godly they seem. It will fail if the change is rooted only in your ideas or personal preferences. Maybe not immediately, but eventually. If it flows from God's heart to the people's hearts, it will endure long after you're gone. Your task as a pastor is not to change people but to create the conditions where God can.

A Biblical Reflection

Ezekiel 36:26 expresses this truth clearly: "I will give you a new heart and put a new spirit within you; I will remove the heart of stone and give you a heart of flesh." The emphasis is unmistakable. God is the one who acts, not the pastor, not the evangelist, and not the church board. Only God can take a hardened heart and make it soft again. Pastors are instruments of transformation, not the agents of it. We are tools in God's hands, not the source of the power. The distinction matters deeply. True change happens only when God's Spirit works within both the pastor and the people simultaneously.

Encouragement for New Pastors

If you are frustrated that people are not changing as quickly as you hoped, pause. That frustration is normal. Every pastor feels it. What you do with that frustration, however, determines your effectiveness. Try to see things from their perspective. Many church members have seen pastors come and go, each with a new vision and new systems. They have watched leaders arrive with grand ideas, make sweeping changes, and then leave, leaving the congregation to pick up the pieces. Why should you be any different? Constant change feels exhausting.

Others have been doing things the same way for decades. That worship style is how they have met God for fifty years. That committee structure is how they have served faithfully for generations. Asking them to abandon what is familiar without clear evidence of God's leading does not just make them uncomfortable; it also undermines their faith. It feels as though you are dismantling their spiritual home.

So what can you do? How do you lead change without forcing it? A couple of things. First, preach before you propose. Let change flow from the pulpit, grounded in God's Word, so people see it as His will and not merely your idea. Spend time teaching the biblical foundation before ever presenting a plan. Let Scripture prepare the soil before you plant the seed. Second, identify the change agents in your congregation. These are the trusted members whose voices carry influence and whose example others follow. They are often the ones who have been there longer than any pastor. Their trust within the church may exceed yours, especially if you are new. Win them first, and they will help you win the rest. And above all, pray. Ask God to change their hearts and yours, because sometimes the heart that needs to change most is the pastor's. Pray not only for cooperation with your plans, but also for alignment with God's will.

Remember that change is necessary, but forced change can harm both the pastor and the people. I have seen pastors burn out from trying to drag congregations into their vision. I have also seen churches wounded by leaders who moved too quickly. Both outcomes can be avoided. Be patient. Be prayerful. Trust God's timing. You cannot change people, but God can. And He will, in His time, not yours.

PART II - LEARNING THE HARD WAY

CHAPTER 4

Balance Begins with Boundaries

One of the myths I once believed was that accessibility defined good leadership. I thought that being available at all times made me a better pastor, more dedicated, and more servant-hearted. One Sabbath, during my pastoral remarks, I made a decision that I would later regret. I gave my phone number to the entire congregation from the pulpit. I wanted every member to know they could reach me whenever they needed to. I wanted them to feel cared for and to know their pastor was only a phone call away. It seemed noble at the time.

Within days, the calls and texts started pouring in. Early morning check-ins. Late-night prayer requests. Weekend questions about church events. Members would call during dinner, during family time, and in the few quiet moments I had to rest. Even when I told them I was unavailable and delegated to others, they would still bypass the structure and contact me directly. "I know you said to call someone else, but I just wanted to talk to you." "I know it's your day off, but this will only take a minute." It never took just a minute.

It did not take long for me to realize that in trying to be everything to everyone, I was becoming nothing to myself. I was exhausted. My marriage was strained. My quiet time with God became almost nonexistent. I had given people unlimited access to me, and they used that access freely, walking into my life whenever they pleased. Every ring and vibration of my phone began to control my life. I felt anxious every time it buzzed. I dreaded opening my messages. The phone that was supposed to keep me connected had made me a prisoner.

I quickly learned that to last in ministry, I had to create balance, and that balance had to begin immediately. I could already feel myself starting to resent the people I was called to serve. That was the moment I realized that balance begins with boundaries.

Boundaries are not about being harsh or unloving. They are about being human. You cannot pour from an empty cup. You cannot shepherd effectively when you are running on fumes. Boundaries protect your ability to serve long-term. You cannot pour into others if you have nothing left to give. Jesus Himself often withdrew to pray, as Luke 5:16 tells us. The Son of God, with infinite capacity, still set boundaries with people. If He needed space away from the crowds, then so do we. And we have far less capacity than He did. Paul said that he became all things to all people (1 Corinthians 9:22), but he never said he was all things to all people all the time. That distinction matters. Flexibility is not the same as constant availability. Adaptation is not the same as having no limits.

I began setting boundaries with my availability. I created a schedule and communicated it clearly. Monday was my day off. Tuesday through Thursday were ministry days. Friday was family day, with no meetings and no calls unless there was an emergency. Saturday was the Sabbath, and Sunday was reserved for meetings and funerals. I started ignoring calls and messages during my off times. It felt wrong at first, as if I were neglecting people, but over time, members learned to respect my humanity. The church did not fall apart. Emergencies were still handled. Life went on.

Boundaries are not only for members. They are also for colleagues and administrators. This is where many new pastors struggle. We are taught to respect authority, and we should, but respect does not mean becoming a doormat. As a new pastor, you may feel pressure to accept every preaching invitation or agree to every request from leadership. You want to prove yourself dependable, eager, and cooperative. I understand that. But I also learned that you cannot preach for everyone. Your first responsibility is to the congregations you have been assigned. Every weekend you spend away from them is a weekend you are not shepherding your own flock.

Be wise about your preaching invitations. Preach only for those who would also preach for you, unless the opportunity clearly aligns with your ministry goals or spiritual growth. If someone constantly asks you to fill their pulpit but never offers to help you in return, that is not partnership; it is exploitation. Do not allow yourself to become anyone's backup plan. Value yourself enough to say no. Your time has value. Your rest has value. Your family deserves your presence.

The same is true with administration. Do not become your administrator's yes-man. Not every request from leadership is reasonable. Not every expectation is biblical. Not every demand is part of your calling. Boundaries communicate respect for yourself and for others. When you respect your limits, you teach others to respect theirs as well. When you have no boundaries, you silently invite people to overstep them, even if they do not mean to. Without boundaries, you will be drained, frustrated, and ineffective. Worse, you will grow bitter toward the very people and calling you once loved. Boundaries protect more than your schedule; they protect your heart.

The Lesson

Ministry's longevity depends on boundaries. Saying no is not a sign of weakness. It is a sign of wisdom. The pastors who last decades in ministry are not the ones who said yes to everything. They're the ones who learned when to say no. The sooner you learn to guard your time, energy, and responsibilities, the more faithfully you will serve. Boundaries are not barriers to ministry. They're the framework that makes sustainable ministry possible.

A Biblical Reflection

Scripture reminds us that even in ministry, rest and withdrawal are necessary. Jesus modeled boundaries by stepping away from the crowds to pray, showing us that uninterrupted access is not godliness but imbalance. He walked away from crowds who wanted more from Him. He prioritized time with the Father over constant availability to people. And He was perfect. Setting boundaries is not selfish. It is stewardship of your life, your family, and your calling. God entrusted you with one body, one mind, one marriage, and one family. How you manage those is how you honor Him. Burning out serves no one.

Encouragement for New Pastors

If you are a new pastor, do not feel guilty about boundaries. Yes, some members may not like them initially. They may complain. They may test them. However, over time, they will respect you more because you set them. Boundaries teach the church that their pastor is not only a shepherd but also a human being, a spouse, a parent, and a friend. Your congregation needs to see your humanity, not just your calling. When you protect your family time, you model healthy priorities for them. When you rest, you permit them to relax too. Boundaries also guard you from being misused by colleagues or taken for granted by administrators. Ministry culture can be toxic when boundaries are absent. Protect yourself. You're not being difficult. You're being wise.

Consider getting a second phone, one for ministry and one for personal use. Turn off the ministry phone during off-hours. Don't even keep it in the same room. The separation creates both physical and psychological space you desperately need. Decide when you are available and when you are not, then communicate it clearly and stick to it consistently. Please put it in the bulletin. Announce it from the pulpit. Please include it in your email signature. Make it clear that members cannot claim they didn't know. Learn to say no, even if it disappoints someone in the moment, because it will preserve your strength for the long haul. Disappointing people occasionally is better than collapsing completely. One protects your ministry; the other ends it.

Remember this: balance in ministry is not something that is discovered; it is something that is cultivated. It is built. And it is built one boundary at a time. Start today. Start small. But start. Your future self will thank you.

CHAPTER 5

Understanding Different Types of Critics

Criticism is unavoidable in ministry. From the moment you step into leadership, people will form opinions, offer feedback, and at times tear down your efforts. You will be criticized for what you do and for what you do not do, for moving too fast or too slow, for preaching too long or not long enough. Some criticism will be fair, some will be biased, and all of it will test you. Some words will cut deeply, while others will be so unreasonable that you can only shake your head. Yet each experience will reveal something about your own heart. I have learned that criticism is not only unavoidable but also necessary. Pastors who cannot handle it rarely grow and develop. Those who learn from it become stronger, wiser, and more effective.

Feedback, even when it is painful, can become a valuable tool for growth. It exposes blind spots you cannot see on your own. It highlights weaknesses you may have overlooked. It provides an opportunity to improve if you are humble enough to accept it. Not all criticism, however, carries the same value. Some is constructive, offered with love and genuine concern, rooted in a desire to see you succeed. Some is destructive, fueled by jealousy or fear, intended to tear you down rather than build you up. Learning to distinguish between them is essential, as failing to do so can break you.

I learned this lesson the hard way, through wounds that still remind me of where I have been. At my first business meeting, before I could even call the meeting to order, a member stood and declared that I could have been her grandson and that her grandson had no business pastoring her. The room went silent. In another instance, my wife and I faced sharp criticism for wearing our wedding bands. Some members were offended, while others defended us, and before long, the issue divided the congregation. A discussion that should have been about mission became an argument over two pieces of jewelry.

I recall organizing a youth program that was filled with praise, music, and energy. Young people from the community attended, many of whom had not set foot in a church in years. We saw lives touched and hearts stirred. I thought we were winning. Instead of celebration, I was called into a meeting with the elders, where every aspect of the program was condemned as inappropriate. The music was too loud, the energy too expressive, and the atmosphere was deemed unfit for sacred space. They wanted it stopped. I was criticized for my preaching style, which was considered too passionate. For my leadership, I was too young. For my appearance, it was too casual, even for asking someone to serve as a church receptionist. The last one is a very funny story.

When I asked a member to manage the church phone, I gave the device to my wife to pass along during the prayer meeting. The following week, I was labeled the most disrespectful pastor they had ever had because I had not handed it over personally. Apparently, having my wife deliver it was an insult.

Criticism came from every side: elders, longtime members, and even visitors. Some of it pierced deeply, especially when I knew how hard I was working. I was giving sixty hours a week, sacrificing family time, and pouring my heart into preaching and pastoral care. Still, for some, it was never enough.

Yet through it all, I discovered a liberating truth. Criticism often reveals more about the critic than about the one being criticized. It offers a window into their heart, their fears, their need for control, and their unresolved pain.

Over time, I realized every church has at least three main types of critics. Learning to identify which type you're dealing with changes everything about how you respond:

1. **The Power Brokers** – Those who criticize because they wish they had your position or believe they could do your job better. They might be elders, deacons, or longtime members who ran things before you arrived. Their criticism is rooted in jealousy, control, or threatened identity. They not only want you to fail; they want you to submit to their vision.

2. **The Constructive Voices** – Those who criticize because they believe in you and genuinely want you to grow. They may not always fully understand your vision, but their feedback stems from a place of love, not malice. Their tone is respectful. Their timing is considerate. They criticize privately, not publicly. These are your most valuable critics.

3. **The Cynics** – Those who criticize because that is simply who they are. They criticized your predecessor. They'll criticize your successor. They are never satisfied and will always find something wrong with the music, the temperature, the sermon length, or the bulletin font. Their criticism isn't

about you. It's their personality. Don't take it personally; don't waste energy trying to convince them.

Knowing which type of critic you are dealing with makes all the difference. Power Brokers require boundaries. Constructive Voices require listening. Cynics require patience, and sometimes, gracious ignoring.

The Lesson

Criticism is not an enemy. It is a teacher, but only if you're willing to learn from it. You must discern whether it will help you grow or discourage you. Not every voice deserves equal weight in your life. When you categorize criticism correctly, you can respond wisely, without becoming bitter or broken. You'll know when to listen carefully, when to set boundaries, and when to let it roll off your back. This discernment protects both your ministry and your mental health.

A Biblical Reflection

Criticism is as old as ministry itself. Moses faced constant complaints from the Israelites, even after God parted the Red Sea and destroyed Pharaoh's army before their eyes. Think about that: God performed the most dramatic miracle in human history, and within days, the people complained about food and water. In the wilderness, they grumbled, wishing they were back in Egypt, longing for the days of slavery (Exodus 16). Their criticism wasn't really about Moses' leadership. It was about their own fears and discomfort. The criticism said more about them than it did about Moses.

Scripture reminds us that our calling is secure regardless of what others say. Critics don't confirm your calling. God does. And what God confirms, no amount of criticism can revoke. God told Jeremiah, 'Before I formed you in the womb, I knew you; before you were born, I set you apart; I appointed you as a prophet to the nations' (Jeremiah 1:5). Notice the timing: before birth, before training, before any human critique, God had already confirmed Jeremiah's calling. Before Jesus performed any miracle and proved Himself to anyone, God declared at His baptism, 'This is my beloved Son, in whom I am well pleased' (Matthew 3:17). Jesus' worth was affirmed before His work began. The same is true for you. God affirms your worth and calling before you ever stood before the critics. You don't need their approval to have value. You don't need their validation to have purpose. God determined your worth and confirmed your calling long before you went to seminary, let alone accepted the call to your current assignment.

Encouragement for New Pastors

If you are crushed by criticism, and at some point, you will be, remember these truths:

Criticism is inevitable. It's coming whether you're a good pastor or a bad one, so don't fear it. Learn from it. The best pastors aren't those who avoid criticism; instead, they are those who welcome it. They're the ones who know how to process it without being destroyed by it.

Not all criticism is destructive. Some will stretch you into becoming a stronger pastor. The criticism that hurts most is the one received when you think you are doing your best. However, don't dismiss it if multiple people say the same thing. Consider it.

God's approval is greater than man's opinion. Your calling was confirmed long before the critics arrived, and it remains secure long after they leave. Let God's voice be louder in your heart than the critics' voices in your ears.

Surround yourself with encouragers. In every church, at least one member will see your effort and say, 'Pastor, you're doing a good job.' Keep them close. Write down their encouragement. Read it when the critics get loud. These voices are just as real as the critical ones. Don't let volume determine validity. Lean on your family. Seek constructive feedback from your spouse or children, people who love you and want you to succeed. Your family's honest feedback, given in love, prepares you to handle the church's input with wisdom rather than defensiveness.

Criticism will sting: sometimes for days, sometimes for years. You must choose whether criticism becomes a wound that festers or a scar that strengthens. Used wisely, it will shape you into a stronger, wiser, and more resilient leader. The pastors with the most profound wisdom are often the ones who've been criticized the most and have learned from it, rather than running from it. Remember: The God who called you does not criticize you. He confirms you. He doesn't tear you down, He builds you up. He doesn't shame you into holiness. He speaks truth in love, and His correction always comes with the strength to change. That's the voice to follow. That's the voice that matters. All the rest is just noise.

CHAPTER 6

Many Leaders Wrestle with Their Own Conversion

Spending time with God sharpens your spiritual discernment. The more you pray, the more clearly you see. Not only what people display in church, but what is taking place in their hearts. Over time, you notice growth or the troubling absence of it among those called to serve. I painfully learned this truth. Titles do not equal transformation.

I once asked Brother Sam to speak one Sabbath, expecting to hear a powerful message from the Word of God. Before I arrived, I had been told that he was a gifted preacher. Instead, he spent nearly fifteen minutes publicly shaming his wife from the pulpit. The congregation sat in silence, stunned. His justification was that God had told him not to marry her, but he disobeyed, and now he lived in regret. Somehow, Brother Sam believed that the pulpit was the right place to confess and air that regret before the church. To hear such a personal attack from the pulpit was not only shocking but deeply sinful. It revealed that something was gravely wrong in his heart.

As I got to know him better, the problems became clearer. When I visited his home, I found no evidence of family worship or Bible study. There was no sign of the fruit of the Spirit in their daily life. During one visit, he and his wife could not even agree on which side of the living room to sit, so she sat on the right and he on the left. The atmosphere was tense and broken.

During one Bible study, while I was teaching about the grace of God, Brother Sam stood up and openly challenged me before the congregation. His words were not questions seeking understanding but outright rejection of the very doctrine he was supposed to uphold. The confrontation was public, disruptive, and revealed a deep-seated theological confusion. Over the course of that year, a pattern emerged. Brother Sam avoided the church's evangelistic work. When I preached, he was absent. When I was away, he appeared and preached. It was no longer about partnership in ministry but about power and control.

His behavior only worsened. On one occasion, he told a church member, in my presence, that she was going to hell for showing favoritism to the pastor and first lady by saving them a piece of cake after a fellowship meal. When I confronted him privately, he refused to apologize. Even when I brought witnesses, he stood his ground without remorse.

All of this confirmed one thing. Brother Sam was struggling with his conversion. Unconverted leaders are not simply difficult. They are dangerous. Their influence can wound believers, discourage seekers, and poison the spiritual life of the church. Left unchecked, they can create an environment where spiritual abuse becomes accepted and normalized.

The Lesson

You cannot assume that every leader is walking closely with God. Ordination certificates do not guarantee conversion, and titles do not confirm calling. Some individuals have accepted leadership roles without first experiencing genuine transformation. You cannot convert them, for that is God's work alone. However, you are called to be their spiritual guide.

Pray for them by name. Model faithfulness with consistency. Point them toward a deeper relationship with Christ through patient teaching and honest, compassionate conversation. Whenever possible, help them grow through mentorship and accountability. When growth proves impossible, replace them by following proper church procedures.

At times, however, neither approach will be practical due to church politics or denominational structures that hinder immediate change. In those moments, you must find another path. Work around the resistance so that the church's mission is not hindered. This often means identifying and nurturing new leaders who are willing to carry the spiritual weight that others have refused to bear.

A Biblical Reflection

Paul illustrates this truth powerfully. Before his conversion in Acts 9, he was zealous, active, and passionate about God. He had impeccable credentials, extensive training, and genuine sincerity. Yet he was unconverted. His efforts, though sincere, were not only misguided but actively harmful.

He persecuted the very church he would later serve. That reminds us that God can and does use even unconverted people for His purposes. But His ultimate goal is always transformation, not just utilization. He doesn't want workers; He wants worshipers. He doesn't want leaders who serve Him out of duty; He wants sons and daughters who serve Him out of love.

Jesus gave us a clear standard: 'By their fruits you will know them' (Matthew 7:20). When a leader's life consistently contradicts the fruit of the Spirit: love, joy, peace, patience, kindness, goodness, faithfulness, gentleness, and self-control, it is a sign that conversion has not yet taken root. One bad day doesn't mean unconverted, but a pattern of spiritual fruitlessness reveals a deeper problem.

Encouragement for New Pastors

There is an unconverted Brother Sam in every church. Sometimes there are several. When you encounter such leaders, the temptation will be to grow bitter, to fight every battle, or to walk away in frustration. I understand that temptation because I have felt it myself. Resist it, not because frustration is wrong, but because bitterness will destroy you faster than any unconverted leader ever could.

Remember that you, too, are on a journey of spiritual growth. There are areas where you still struggle and seasons when your own conversion is tested. Just as God is patient with you, He calls you to show patience to others. This does not mean tolerating spiritual abuse, but it does mean approaching unconverted leaders with compassion rather than contempt.

Pray for their conversion. Pray for their families. Pray for their hearts to soften toward God. Offer specific prayers, not vague ones. Prayer not only invites God to work in their lives but also guards your heart from resentment. It is difficult to despise someone you are sincerely praying for. Over time, prayer smooths the sharp edges of disappointment and reminds you that the church belongs to God, not to you. These unconverted leaders are His responsibility. Your role is to be faithful, to speak truth, and to trust God with what you cannot control.

Do not let unconverted leaders distract you from your mission. Focus on those who are willing to grow, even if they are few in number. Pour into them, encourage them, and build with them. God often does His most significant work through a small, faithful remnant rather than an entire congregation. Quality matters more than quantity when it comes to spiritual leadership.

You are also not meant to carry this burden alone. Find strength in fellowship with other pastors who understand these struggles. Seek mentors who have endured similar challenges and can offer perspective. Maintain friendships outside of your congregation where you can speak freely and honestly. These relationships remind you of your calling when ministry feels heavy. They help you see clearly when your emotions cloud your judgment.

Take comfort in knowing that this struggle is not new. Moses faced rebellion from Korah. Samuel grieved over his sons' corruption. Paul battled false apostles in the very churches he founded. Yet through it all, God remained faithful, and He will remain faithful to you.

Unconverted leaders may slow the work, create obstacles, and cause deep heartache, but they cannot stop the mission of God. In that evangelistic series where Brother Sam refused to help, people were still baptized. The gospel still advances because the gates of hell will never prevail against the church Christ is building. Stay faithful. Stay prayerful. Keep your eyes on the One who called you, not on Brother Sam.

PART III - WHEN THE WELL RUNS DRY

CHAPTER 7

You Will Face Dry Seasons

Sermons flow with ease. Prayer feels alive. Ministry bears fruit everywhere you turn. These are the seasons that remind you why you answered the call. But they do not last forever. Then come the dry seasons, when prayer feels empty, sermons feel hollow, and even God seems silent. These seasons test you in ways that flourishing seasons never can.

I have lived through those dry seasons. Sabbaths arrived when I was scheduled to preach, yet no word came. I prayed, but nothing. I studied, but still nothing. I sought God's face with desperation, and heaven remained quiet. The silence was deafening. I continued pouring myself into ministry, visiting the sick, counseling those in need, preaching each Sabbath, and leading every board meeting. But inwardly, I felt empty. I was giving from a well that had already run dry.

Over time, I began to realize that my humanity played a role in it. Dry seasons often came when I was overwhelmed, stressed, or burned out. I was running too fast, carrying too much, and saying yes to everything. My body and spirit were trying to warn me, but I was not listening. I kept putting out fires that didn't require my presence, stepping into conflicts I should have delegated, and responding to crises that weren't truly crises. I was trying to be all things to all people, available at every hour, solving every problem that came my way. Running on fumes became normal.

At other times, the dryness came from a more profound confusion. I was mistaking pastoral work for spiritual growth. I thought ministry activity equaled vitality. It does not. I thought preaching to others meant I was feeding myself. It does not. I thought praying for others meant I was praying for myself. It does not. Pastoring is not the same as being pastored by God. You can perform all the work of ministry and still be spiritually starving.

In those moments, I had to stop and ask the hard questions. Was I truly resting, or just collapsing between crises? Was I spending time with God for myself, not merely for sermon preparation? Was I giving out more than I was taking in? The answer, every time, was yes. I was spiritually depleted.

The Lesson

Dry seasons cannot be avoided. They are part of ministry and part of life. Every pastor encounters them, some more than once. How you respond to these seasons will shape your growth far more than the flourishing ones ever could.

God requires faithfulness in both abundance and in times of drought. Ministry is not measured by visible results but by steadfast endurance. God did not call you to constant productivity. He called you to remain faithful, to endure, and to stand firm even when you feel empty, especially when you feel empty.

A Biblical Reflection

Psalm 13 has often encouraged me in dry seasons. David cries out, 'How long, Lord? Will you forget me forever? How long will you hide your face from me?' (Psalm 13:1). Notice what David doesn't do. He doesn't pretend everything is fine. He doesn't fake spiritual strength. He honestly laments. He is speaking, but God seems silent. That is the reality of a dry season. And God doesn't punish David for his honesty. Yet even in that silence, David ends with trust: 'But I trust in your unfailing love' (Psalm 13:5). Notice the word 'but.' It's a turning point. The lament is honest, but it doesn't end in despair. Dry seasons test our commitment to God just as much as flourishing seasons do. They reveal whether we love God for what He gives us or for who He is.

The woman at the well in John 4 also comes to mind. She arrived empty at noon, the hottest part of the day, seeking water from a well that could never truly satisfy. She left filled because she encountered the Living Water. The well she had been drawing from her entire life was never meant to sustain her. Dry seasons remind us we cannot survive on our own; we must return repeatedly to the Source of life.

Encouragement for New Pastors

If you are facing your first dry season, do not feel guilty. I know that you probably do. Most pastors assume that dryness means failure, as if it were evidence of hidden sin or disqualification. But dryness does not mean you have lost your calling. It does not mean you should leave the ministry. It does not mean you are unfit for the task. It simply means you are human. Even Elijah faced his own dry season. God is not finished with you. In fact, He may be using this time to slow you down before you burn out, to teach you dependence before you collapse under the weight of self-reliance, and to reset your priorities before you sacrifice what matters most on the altar of ministry. Dry seasons are often God's mercy, not His punishment.

When you feel dry, return to the Source. Pray more, but pray differently. Stop praying only for your congregation and begin praying for yourself. Study more, but study for your soul, not just for your sermons. Read passages that speak to you personally. And rest more. Truly rest. Evaluate your stress honestly. Write down what is weighing you down and ask yourself which of those things are yours to carry. Step back from unnecessary burdens. Say no. Delegate. Let some things fail. Find hobbies or simple joys that clear your mind and quiet your heart. Go for walks, play music, read, garden, or cook. Do something that has nothing to do with ministry. When your spirit is rested, you can hear God again. Sometimes He speaks loudest when you stop trying so hard to listen.

Most of all, remember that dry seasons do not last forever. They feel endless when you are in them, but they always end. Seasons change. Spring follows winter. Rain follows drought. This will pass.

Your calling is not proven when you feel strong. Anyone can be faithful when everything is going well and every sermon resonates. Your calling is proven when you remain faithful despite feeling weak, when you preach with nothing to give, and when you visit the sick, even though you feel empty yourself. When you keep shepherding even as you long to be shepherded. Dryness is not the end of your ministry. It is the soil where God often grows new roots. The deepest roots form in the driest ground.

Do not compare your dry season to someone else's flourishing one. Social media often showcases pastors whose churches are thriving and whose ministries appear effortless. Do not measure your winter by their spring. You are in a different season, facing a different assignment, walking a different road. God is not doing the same work in you that He is doing in them. Trust His process for you.

And if your dry season stretches beyond a year, deepens into despair, or makes daily life unbearable, seek help. Talk to a counselor, see a doctor, speak with a mentor. Spiritual dryness is normal. Clinical depression is a medical condition that needs treatment. Know the difference. There is no shame in getting help when the dryness becomes too heavy to bear alone.

CHAPTER 8

Prioritizing Preparation for Worship Leadership

Standing in the pulpit unprepared is a terrible feeling. The gaps show, transitions become awkward, and the flow feels disjointed. You can sense the congregation's confusion. Those moments often came after a hectic week when I had not taken enough time to plan the service. In larger churches, a team can absorb those gaps. The worship leader carries the music, the deacons manage logistics, and an associate pastor can adapt quickly. In smaller churches, however, the responsibility rests almost entirely on you. Every gap shows. Every lapse disrupts. And rightly so, because every pastor is a worship leader.

This does not mean that you must do everything yourself. It means that you must carry a clear vision of what worship should look like, sound like, and feel like for your congregation. You set the tone. You establish the flow. You create the atmosphere where God can meet His people. You stand between God and the people, serving as the conduit through which worship flows. When that conduit is blocked by poor preparation, worship suffers, and the congregation senses it immediately.

When I entered worship unprepared, I felt it instantly. Transitions were awkward, elements were forgotten, instructions were unclear, and the rhythm of the service was broken. Even my preaching reflected it. I could still deliver a sermon—the words were there—but it lacked depth and anointing because I had not taken the time to prepare my heart or the worship experience. I was performing rather than leading people into the presence of God.

The Lesson

Good worship flows through the leader. You cannot expect your congregation to give what you have not prepared yourself to give. You cannot lead people into a place you have not already been. Your public worship is an overflow of your private worship. If you have not spent time with God during the week, if your devotional life is dry, it is hypocrisy to expect your members to experience what you have not. They will sense the emptiness. Congregations can discern when their pastor is preaching from personal experience rather than secondhand information. Preparation for worship is not optional. It is essential.

A Biblical Reflection

The Old Testament priesthood illustrates this truth clearly. The priest was responsible for stewarding the worship experience. They did not sing every song or offer every prayer, but they set the order and ensured everything was adequately prepared. Worship flowed through them, and their preparation determined the quality of the congregation's encounter with God. A poorly prepared priest meant a poorly led service, and sometimes, the results were far worse.

In Leviticus, Nadab and Abihu offered unauthorized fire before the Lord because they failed to follow the prescribed order, and the result was fatal. Similarly, a poorly planned worship service reflects a pastor who has not taken the time to prepare. The consequences may not be fatal, but they are real. People leave unchanged. God's name is dishonored. Seekers are turned away.

Jesus reminds us in John 4:24 that true worshipers must worship in spirit and in truth. Spirit requires private devotion. You cannot lead in the Spirit if you have not been walking in the Spirit throughout the week. Truth requires careful planning. You cannot teach truth if you have not studied truth. Both are necessary. One without the other produces false worship.

Encouragement for New Pastors

Preparation must be holistic. It touches every area of your life. Spiritually, spend the week in communion with God. Not just on Thursday when you prepare the sermon, but daily. Listen for His word for His people. Ask what God is trying to say to this specific congregation in this particular season. Physically, rest. Get enough sleep on Friday night. Do not stay up late preparing what you should have prepared earlier in the week. Preaching and leading worship cannot be done well when you are exhausted. Your body affects your spirit. Fatigue weakens discernment, and weariness drains patience.

Emotionally, open yourself to God's grace so you can extend it to others. If you are still carrying bitterness from last week's board meeting, it will show in worship. If you harbor resentment toward a critical member, it will color your tone. Deal with your own heart before you stand before the congregation. Wounded leaders create wounded worship.

Logistically, plan the service with intention. Whether with a committee, a trusted elder, or even alone, write it down. Know the order. Prepare transitions. Anticipate needs. Have backup plans for technology failures. Think through every moment from the opening song to the benediction. Details matter.

Do not cheat your members by entering worship unprepared. They sacrificed to be there. They arranged childcare, drove through traffic, and gave up Saturday morning rest. They came hungry for God. Do not serve them empty plates because you were too busy to prepare. A little planning is always better than none.

Set a weekly schedule for worship preparation. Monday for planning the order, Tuesday for selecting music, Wednesday for sermon development, Thursday for finalizing details, Friday for personal devotion and rest. Whatever system works for you, write it down and follow it. If the workload becomes too heavy, delegate tasks to those you have trained and can trust. But never delegate the responsibility of worship leadership itself.

Remember, worship is the sacred meeting between humanity and divinity. Your job is not to feed the people, because only God can do that. Your responsibility is to create the environment where God can meet His people. You prepare the table. God provides the feast. You open the door. God enters the room. But if the table is unprepared and the door is locked because you neglected preparation, the congregation leaves hungry.

Never forget this: you can only take people to places in worship where you have already been. If you have not met God privately, you cannot introduce Him publicly. You cannot lead others into worship if you have not experienced worship yourself. If your heart has not been prepared, you cannot prepare the hearts of others. Authenticity cannot be faked. The anointing cannot be manufactured. Preparation is not optional. It is essential.

CHAPTER 9

Pastoring is Not the Same as Your Walk

Pastoring can kill your walk with God. I discovered this the hard way. Preaching sermons, visiting members, chairing meetings, and counseling families are all sacred work; yet, none of these activities automatically means that I am walking with God. In fact, they often became substitutes for walking with Him. There were times when I was so busy pastoring that my own devotional life was neglected. I would wake up in the morning, reach for my phone before my Bible, and feel the weight of unread texts and voicemails. Before I could pray, I was already solving problems. Before breakfast, someone was calling about a crisis. Before bed, I was rehearsing tomorrow's responsibilities instead of praying. I was running from hospital visits to counseling sessions, from church repairs to Bible studies, from board meetings to evangelistic planning, from conference calls to crisis interventions, from weddings to funerals. The calendar was full, but my soul was empty.

From the outside, it looked like success. Conference leaders praised my work. Members appreciated my availability. By any measure of productivity, I would have received an A. But God does not grade on productivity. He measures faithfulness, and I was failing the only test that mattered. There were mornings when I skipped personal devotion, not occasionally but regularly. Mornings became filled with routine busyness rather than sacred encounter. Evenings came when I collapsed into bed, too tired to talk to God and too drained to listen. I told myself God understood. He did, but understanding does not mean approval.

I had information, volumes of sermon notes, commentaries, and theological knowledge, but no inspiration. I had a schedule, but lacked the strength to keep it. I had activity but no anointing. I had become a religious professional running on empty. When moments arose that required spiritual power, whether praying for the sick, counseling families in crisis, or standing in the pulpit, I realized that I was ministering from a place of emptiness. The prayers felt hollow. The counsel felt mechanical. The sermons sounded like lectures. I was going through the motions, performing the role, but there was no power, no presence, no anointing.

The truth is that pastoring can deceive you. It is one of the most dangerous traps in ministry. Because the work is sacred and involves handling holy things and constantly speaking about God, it can easily be mistaken for a personal walk with God. You can become so busy working for Him that you forget to be with Him. You can prepare sermons for others and never let the Word reach your own heart.

I have spent hours exegeting passages, analyzing Greek, consulting commentaries, and crafting outlines that inspired congregations. Yet, I never stopped to ask, "What is God saying to me through this text?" The Word became a tool for ministry rather than food for my soul. I prayed for others but rarely prayed for myself. I interceded for the sick, the hurting, the lost, and the struggling, yet when it came to my own brokenness and spiritual hunger, I had nothing left. The intercessor had no one interceding on his behalf.

I spoke about God multiple times each week through sermons, Bible studies, counseling sessions, and prayer meetings. His name was constantly on my lips, yet a personal conversation with Him was rare. I had become a spokesman without a relationship, a representative who had lost connection with headquarters. The greatest danger in ministry is believing that activity proves spirituality. You start to think that because you are preaching, you must be spiritual. Because you are praying for others, your prayer life must be strong. Because you are leading worship, you must also worship. All of that is false. Activity is not intimacy. Busyness is not devotion. Ministry is not relationship.

The Lesson

Pastoring is not the same as knowing God. Write that down and place it somewhere you can see every day. Never confuse your vocation with your devotion. They may overlap, but they are distinct. One is what you do. The other is who you are. You were never called to be more vocationally committed than you are devotionally connected. When your ministry becomes greater than your relationship with God, you are building on sand. When your public calling overshadows your private communion, you are walking toward ruin.

It is possible to be a great pastor and a poor Christian. I have seen it happen. Influential preachers with lifeless prayer lives. Skilled leaders with empty souls. Successful church builders whose families are falling apart. The last thing you want is to work for a God you barely know, to represent someone you rarely spend time with, or to lead others to a place where you no longer dwell.

A Biblical Reflection

When Moses encountered God at the burning bush, he was already busy tending sheep. It was legitimate work, even ministry in its own way. Yet God stopped him and said, "Take off your sandals, for the place where you are standing is holy ground" (Exodus 3:5). God interrupted the work to invite him into worship. The work had to pause so that worship could begin. The same principle applies to pastors today. Ministering must pause to allow worship to begin. You can be busy doing things for God while neglecting time with God.

Paul warned Timothy about those who "have a form of godliness but deny its power" (2 Timothy 3:5). Pastors cannot afford to fall into that category, yet we are the most vulnerable to it. We have all the outward forms: preaching, praying, leading worship, studying Scripture. However, when these become professional activities rather than personal encounters, we are left with the form but not the power. A sermon without the Spirit is just a lecture. A prayer without power is only a recital. Counseling without anointing becomes simple advice. Leadership without God's presence is mere management.

Ministry requires more than performance; it requires presence. The presence of God must first dwell within the pastor. Jesus modeled this perfectly. After long days of preaching, healing, and teaching, He often withdrew to lonely places to pray (Luke 5:16). Notice that it says "often." This was not occasional. It was His pattern, His rhythm, His discipline. If the Son of God, who was always connected to the Father, needed solitude after ministry, how much more do we who are prone to spiritual disconnection?

Without that rhythm of retreat and renewal, ministry becomes mechanical. Sermons sound repetitive. Prayers lose their life. Counseling becomes routine. And the pastor becomes spiritually bankrupt. You can be bankrupt in ministry while everyone thinks you are spiritually rich. The congregation sees the activity. Only you know the account is empty.

Encouragement for New Pastors

If you are new in ministry, aim to spend more time with God than you spend working for Him. Track it if you must. Write down how many hours you spend on ministry tasks, then write down how many hours you spend in personal devotion. If the first number is significantly higher than the second, you are heading for trouble. Schedule your devotional time as deliberately as you schedule meetings and visits. Put it in your calendar. Set alarms. Treat it as the most important appointment of your day. Protect those moments with the same urgency you protect appointments with key members, or better yet, protect them more fiercely, because time with God is more important than time with anyone else.

Build prayer into your rhythm. Not just spontaneous prayers in passing or quick prayers before meals and meetings, but scheduled, focused moments that anchor your day. Pray in the morning before you check your phone. Pray at midday before lunch. Pray in the evening before bed. Make prayer the bookends of your day, not the footnotes.

Find accountability. If you are married, give your spouse permission to ask you directly, "Did you spend time with God today?" Not to shame you, but to remind you. Let them interrupt your busyness and ask, "When was the last time you had real time with God?" If you are single, consider finding a trusted colleague or mentor who can check in with you on a weekly basis about your devotional life. Not superficially, but intentionally. What are you reading? What is God saying to you? How is your soul? Ministry will always tempt you to replace devotion with vocation. The urgent will crowd out the important. The crisis will feel more pressing than communion. Resist that temptation. Say no to ministry tasks if they mean saying no to God. Cancel a meeting if it protects your time with Him. Your first calling is not to the church. It is to Christ.

When you stand before your congregation, your power will not come from eloquence, polish, or education. It comes from one place: the depth of your private time with God. Congregations can feel the difference. They may not have the words for it, but they know when a pastor speaks from overflow rather than from notes. What you pour into others must first be poured into you. If you minister from an empty cup, you will eventually burn out, grow bitter, or collapse under the weight of expectations. I have seen it happen. Faithful pastors who grew cynical. Passionate leaders who turned cold. Effective ministers who quit altogether. Not because they lost their calling, but because they lost connection with the One who called them. But if you minister from overflow, the Spirit will sustain you. You will preach with fresh anointing, counsel with wisdom, and lead with clarity. You will endure hardships that would break others, not because you are stronger, but because you are connected to the Source.

Not every pastor will make it to heaven. That is a sobering truth we rarely speak aloud. There will be influential preachers, effective leaders, and successful church builders who hear Jesus say, "I never knew you." Not because they did not work for Him, but because they never walked with Him. They replaced devotion with vocation. They confused the ministry about God with the relationship with God. Do not let that be your story. Your calling is not just to work for God but to walk with Him. Pastoring is your assignment. Walking with God is your salvation. Do not confuse the two. One day, the work will come to an end. The meetings will stop. The sermons will cease. The counseling sessions will conclude. But your relationship with Christ will last forever. What matters most is not how many people you pastor, but whether you know the Chief Shepherd personally. That relationship is everything.

CHAPTER 10

God Uses Ministry to Save Pastors Too

For years, I dismissed the idea that God uses ministry to save pastors. I had often heard it repeated at conferences, in conversations with older pastors, and in denominational gatherings. Every time I heard it, I rolled my eyes. It sounded like a convenient excuse to dress up personal struggles in spiritual language. I told myself that was just something struggling pastors said to justify their problems. I told myself that God could save us through any means, and ministry was no different; it was just another context for sanctification. That changed once I began pastoring. Pastoring, not theorizing about it. The truth hit me within months.

It did not take long for me to realize that the statement was very true, painfully true. God does use ministry as one of His primary means of saving pastors. It is not the only means, but it is a deliberate and specific tool in His hands for our sanctification. There were moments when I was deeply frustrated with my members, convinced they were stiff-necked, rebellious, and unwilling to listen. They ignored biblical counsel, resisted necessary change, complained about everything, and fought over trivial matters. In those moments, God stopped me. Not audibly, but clearly. He reminded me that I looked the same way to Him. I was stubborn when He called me to obedience. I was resistant when He asked me to change. I did not always follow instructions, even when they were clear. The same frustration I felt toward my members was the same frustration God felt toward me. The ministry became a mirror, showing me the flaws of others and the flaws within myself. Whenever I counseled someone about gossip, I heard my own loose tongue. Every time I preached about forgiveness, I remembered the grudges I was holding. Whenever I challenged someone about their prayer life, I felt a deep sense of my own emptiness. Ministry exposed me to myself.

It dawned on me that God had not placed me in ministry only because of my gifts or talents. That realization was humbling. I thought I was in ministry because I was qualified and had something to offer. But God put me here because He wanted me to confront myself. Working with people whose struggles reflected my own forced me to recognize my desperate need for His grace. Ministry drove me into prayer, real prayer, not just professional prayer. I found myself kneeling, not preparing sermons but crying out for help. It deepened my understanding, not just for sermon preparation, but also for personal growth and survival. It forced me to spend more time with God because I knew the assignment was bigger than me. Much bigger.

Over time, I realized that the real goal of ministry was not simply to make me a better preacher, leader, or pastor. God was not primarily concerned with my competence. He was concerned with my character. Ministry was not about making me effective. It was about making me whole, making me holy, and making me more like Jesus. God was shaping me to be a better follower before becoming a better leader, a better Christian before becoming a better pastor, and a more faithful representative of Him before becoming a more effective minister. The order matters. Character before competence. Being before doing. Ministry was not just about saving others. It was about keeping me from destroying myself by becoming proud, cold, and self-righteous. Ministry was God's protection for me, His way of keeping me humble, dependent, and broken in the right ways. The ministry was saving me.

The Lesson

When you accept the call to ministry, you are giving God full access to your life. Full access. No locked doors. No hidden rooms. That is a dangerous commitment if you are not prepared, because God will hold you to it. He will use every tool at His disposal to shape you, and ministry is one of His most effective tools. He will use it not only as a platform for service but also as a workshop for your spiritual growth and sanctification. Sometimes the workshop feels more like a forge, hot, painful, and relentless. Yet forges produce strength that workshops cannot.

Ministry exposes your weaknesses in ways nothing else can. You cannot hide in ministry. Your character flaws surface in conflict. Your insecurities emerge when you are criticized. Your pride shows when you are ignored. Ministry confronts all of it without mercy. What may appear to be God preparing you for leadership is often God preparing you for eternal life. Leadership is temporary. Your role as a pastor will one day come to an end. But your salvation is eternal. God cares more about your salvation than your sermon series, more about your character than your church growth, and more about saving you than making you successful.

A Biblical Reflection

Paul's testimony in 2 Corinthians has always been a deep source of encouragement to me. Here was one of the greatest apostles the church had ever known. He was a powerful preacher, a profound theologian, an effective evangelist, a church planter, and a miracle worker. Yet he admitted to carrying a thorn in the flesh. Something that weakened him. Something that would not go away. Three times he pleaded with God to remove it, and God said no. But He did not just say no. He explained why: "My grace is sufficient for you, for my power is made perfect in weakness" (2 Corinthians 12:9). The thorn stayed because Paul needed it.

The word "thorn" carries the sense of a stake, as if God had driven it deep into Paul's life to hold him steady like a tent peg driven into the ground. Without it, Paul might have been blown away by pride. He might have relied too heavily on his knowledge, his eloquence, or his success in ministry. The thorn was mercy, not punishment. It reminded him daily that he, too, needed the same grace he preached. Every time it hurt, Paul remembered his dependence on God. Every time he felt weak, he leaned more on divine strength. The thorn was God's way of protecting him from becoming what he warned others against: self-sufficient, proud, and reliant on his own ability.

That truth applies to every pastor. The struggles that frustrate you, the difficult members who test your patience, the financial pressure that drives you to prayer, the criticism that humbles you, and the weaknesses that keep you dependent are not punishments. They are protection. These are the thorns God uses to keep you near Him. Paul warned that it is possible to preach to others and still become a castaway. You can be sound in doctrine but lost in soul. You can be effective in ministry but disqualified from the kingdom. You can lead others to salvation while neglecting your own spiritual growth. That thought terrified Paul, and it should terrify us as well.

Ministry is God's way of preventing that from happening by continually bringing the pastor back to the cross. Back to your own need for grace. Back to your own brokenness. Back to dependence. Every difficult member, every exhausting week, every humbling failure points you back to where it all began, the cross of Christ, where grace never runs out, and where you still belong.

Encouragement for New Pastors

If you are a young pastor, do not believe that ministry is only about saving others. I know that is what you thought when you entered ministry. I thought it too. But God does not need you to save anyone. He does not need your gifts, your education, or your abilities. He is God. He can call out rocks if necessary. He can use donkeys to speak His word. He does not need you, but He has invited you to be a part of this work. Not because He needs you, but because you need it.

While you save others, He is saving you. While you minister to them, He is ministering to you.

Your sermons, counseling, and leadership are not just for your congregation. They are also for you. Every time you preach repentance, God is calling you to repent. Every time you teach about forgiveness, He reminds you who you need to forgive. Whenever you counsel someone about their marriage, He shows you where yours needs improvement. Ministry is God's curriculum for your growth and sanctification. Whenever you urge someone to surrender, God encourages you to do the same. Whenever you remind the church to trust, He asks, "Do you trust Me with this situation?" Every time you call people to repentance, God calls you as well. The message you preach to others, He is preaching to you. The question is, are you listening?

Do not grow arrogant. That is one of ministry's most dangerous temptations. When people praise your preaching, when the church grows, and when your counsel brings healing, arrogance whispers, "You are good at this." Do not listen. Do not let your gifts convince you that ministry is about performance. It is not. The highest calling of ministry is not to display your talents but to surrender yourself as a vessel in God's hands. Not a decorated vessel. Not a talented vessel. Just a surrendered one. Empty enough for Him to fill. Broken enough for Him to use. Dependent enough to give Him glory.

Let the ministry humble you. Stop fighting the humiliation. Let it shape you. Stop resisting the process. Let it sanctify you. Stop trying to arrive. You are still being formed. Ministry is doing precisely what God intends it to do. It is exposing your weakness so that you will depend on His strength. It is revealing your sin so you will seek His grace. It is breaking your self-sufficiency so you will trust His provision.

And never forget this: before God uses you to save others, He uses ministry to save you. The struggles you face in pastoring are not random. They are not punishment. They are not evidence of failure. They are God's way of molding you into His image. The same God who is redeeming your congregation is redeeming you. One sermon at a time. One trial at a time. One tear at a time. One prayer at a time. Ministry is not only your calling. It is God's instrument for your salvation.

CHAPTER 11

Rest is Essential

Geography became my enemy. Four churches were scattered across the Mississippi Delta. One was twenty-eight miles away. Another fifty-six. Another sixty-eight. The farthest, seventy-six miles one way. Rural roads. Small towns. Long drives. Every week, I logged hundreds of miles. During one two-week evangelistic meeting, I drove at least 170 miles each day, a 152-mile round trip, for fourteen straight days. Later, I ran another two-week campaign, covering sixty to sixty-eight miles one way every day. By the end, I was completely drained. Not tired, but burned out. There is a difference.

There were days when I caught myself napping behind the wheel from sheer fatigue. Eyes closing on the highway. Head nodding and crossing the center line. I could have killed myself or someone else. Still, I pressed on, believing the mission would fall apart if I stopped. I was wrong, but too tired to realize it. The truth was sobering. Sometimes the work does not need to be done right away. Sometimes you have to let the ball drop so others recognize their responsibility in ministry. That realization set me free. Not everything is urgent. Not everything depends on you. The mission will survive if you rest.

After one exhausting campaign, I desperately longed for some well-needed recovery. I tried to find someone to fill the pulpit for one Sabbath. I called colleagues. I reached out to conference leaders. I asked my elders. No one was available, or perhaps not willing. Some said they were not capable. Others did not want the responsibility. A few said no without explanation. So I preached, even when I had nothing left to give. Running on empty, preaching from exhaustion instead of anointing. One Sabbath, I was so weary that I could barely finish the sermon. My voice was weak. My thoughts scattered. I forgot points mid-sentence. The congregation could see it. I could feel their concern. It was humiliating.

The following week, I tried again, but something terrifying happened: I had not heard from God. My mind was too tired to focus, too drained to discern His voice. Heaven was silent, not because God had stopped speaking, but because I was too exhausted to listen. I had to preach without a word from the Lord. Standing in the pulpit with nothing. That moment broke me. I realized I would not last in ministry if I did not learn to rest.

The Lesson

Take care of your body so that your body can take care of you. This is not optional. It is not self-indulgence. It is stewardship. If you neglect yourself, your ministry will be short-lived. Your body will eventually force you to stop. The only question is whether you stop voluntarily through rest or involuntarily through collapse.

The ministry will always have more work than you can finish. Always. The list will never end. The needs will never stop. Some problems existed before you arrived and will remain long after you are gone. You are not responsible for fixing everything. You are responsible for being faithful. And you cannot be faithful if you are physically or emotionally destroyed.

Do not sacrifice yourself on the altar of ministry. This is not hyperbole. Some pastors have died from stress-related illnesses because they refused to rest. Heart attacks. Strokes. Burnout that led to despair and even suicide. These are not dramatic exaggerations. They are the sobering reality of unchecked overwork.

Rest is not a luxury. It is obedience. It is stewardship.

A Biblical Reflection

Scripture repeatedly emphasizes the importance of rest. John writes, "Beloved, I wish above all things that you may prosper and be in health, even as your soul prospers" (3 John 1:2). Notice the order. Health is mentioned before soul prosperity. Physical well-being matters to God. Your body is not separate from your spiritual life. They are deeply connected.

Health involves more than exercise and diet. It includes adequate rest. Sleep. Sabbath. Vacation. Time off. Without these, the body and mind eventually break down. Not might. Will. Your body keeps score. You can neglect rest for a time, but eventually the bill must be paid.

Jesus said, "Come to Me, all you who are weary and heavy laden, and I will give you rest" (Matthew 11:28). This is an invitation, not a suggestion. Rest is not just physical. It is spiritual. It is one of God's greatest gifts to those who labor in His vineyard. To refuse rest is to refuse that gift.

Rest is woven into the very fabric of creation. After six days of work, God Himself rested. Not because He was weary, but because He was establishing a pattern for human life. A divine rhythm. To ignore that rhythm is to live outside of God's design.

Sabbath itself stands as a weekly reminder of this truth. God calls us to worship and enter into both divine and physical rest that renews body and soul. Just as manna stopped on the Sabbath to teach Israel to trust God's provision, so God still calls us to stop striving and trust that He can sustain His work without us; the church will survive without you for a day. The mission will move forward without your constant presence. God is big enough to uphold His work while you rest.

Encouragement for New Pastors

An older pastor once told me, "Ministry is not a sprint. It is a marathon." He was right. It often feels like a sprint because the needs seem urgent, the expectations are heavy, and the demands are endless. But if you try to run a marathon at sprint speed, you will not last. The pressure to do everything, be everywhere, and prove your calling through constant busyness is real, but that pace will destroy your body, your marriage, your children, and even your faith. You will lose what matters most while trying to prove that you can handle everything.

Rest is Essential

Take your rest without guilt. Rest is not laziness or selfishness; it is a form of self-care and self-respect. It is biblical. Some members will not understand your humanity. They may criticize you for taking a day off or compare you to previous pastors who "never rested." Let them talk. Their opinions will not matter when your health fails. Listen to your body. Steward it well.

Choose a weekly rest day beyond the Sabbath, because the Sabbath is not a day off for pastors. It is sacred labor—all that preaching, leading, counseling, and serving. Though spiritually rich, it is physically and emotionally draining. If Sabbath is your only rest day, you have no rest day. Many pastors take Monday to recover from the weekend, but whatever day you choose, protect it. Add it to your calendar, block off the time, notify your team, and consider turning off your phone if necessary. Treat it as a sacred appointment with yourself, your family, and your God.

Do not sacrifice your health or family on the altar of ministry. I have seen pastors work themselves to death, neglect their marriages until they crumble, and miss their children's entire childhoods. The church will replace you quickly when you are gone, but your family will carry the pain for life. Missed birthdays, broken promises, and emotional absence leave scars that do not fade. Your family will remember what you chose long after the church has forgotten you.

Rest also protects your mind. Stress, anxiety, and depression often grow from unrelieved exhaustion. You cannot counsel, pray, or preach your way out of burnout. The solution is rest, real, consistent, extended rest. Exhausted pastors become harmful to themselves, their families, and their congregations. They preach in anger, counsel without compassion, lead without vision, and live resentful of their calling. Rest is not optional. It is survival.

Take care of yourself because you cannot pastor well if you are unwell. You cannot lead from emptiness or pour from an empty cup. Rest is not wasted time; it is preparation time. It renews your strength, sharpens your perspective, and restores your joy. A rested pastor is a stronger preacher, a wiser leader, and a more compassionate shepherd.

PART IV – BEYOND THE PULPIT

CHAPTER 12

Making Hard Decisions is Unavoidable

Three or four people. That was my entire congregation at one church. Not three or four hundred, just three or four. On some Sabbaths, only two attended. It was one of the most challenging seasons in my early ministry. This was the same church from my first week, the one with the unpaid electric bill. They had no money in their account, the city had repossessed their trash can for unpaid fees, and the water was about to be turned off. The financial crisis was only the surface problem. The deeper issue was spiritual. Upon reviewing their records, the situation worsened. The church had lost over 90 percent of its membership in a decade. No baptisms. No visitors. No children. Only a few aging saints watching their church die slowly.

Faced with this reality, we had to determine whether the church could be revived or needed to close. It was a decision I never wanted to make. As a young pastor, I did not feel qualified even to suggest closure. Seasoned pastors had warned me not to let a church die under my watch. But someone had to decide. My wife and I worked tirelessly with the members. We cleaned the building from top to bottom, repaired pews, hosted youth programs, and partnered with a nearby congregation for joint services. We invited the community. But nothing changed. No growth. No life. The members were not evangelistic. They had no interest in outreach, no desire to invite neighbors, and no willingness to adapt worship for visitors. They wanted things precisely as they had always been, even if that meant death. And so, the decline continued.

Eventually, after prayer, consultation with conference leaders, and multiple meetings with the members, we made the difficult decision to close the church. It was not popular. One member was furious and refused to transfer her membership. But it was the right decision. By merging with another congregation, we built something more substantial: more resources, renewed energy, deeper worship, and genuine outreach. Within a year, the new congregation had experienced baptisms, welcomed new members, and was on the path to a new life. The mission continued. That is what mattered.

The Lesson

Pastoral leadership often requires making difficult decisions, especially those that are unpopular. You will never lead if you wait for universal agreement. You may manage, but you will not lead. Every choice must be filtered through one question: Does this serve the mission? If it does not advance the gospel, strengthen the church, or align with God's calling, it is not worth pursuing. As my friend Dr. Michael Harvey often reminds me, "Lead by principle, not by popularity." Those words have steadied me many times.

A Biblical Reflection

Scripture is filled with leaders who made unpopular but necessary choices. Jesus told His disciples, "If anyone will not receive you, shake the dust off your feet and move on" (Matthew 10:14). No guilt. No hesitation. Move on. Joshua declared, "As for me and my house, we will serve the Lord" (Joshua 24:15), even when the nation wavered. He did not take a vote; he led with conviction. That is leadership; decisions grounded in principle, not popularity. True leaders remember that their allegiance is to God's mission, not human approval. The moment you prioritize applause over obedience, you cease to be a pastor and become a politician.

Encouragement for New Pastors

If you are a young pastor facing a hard decision, I know the weight. The sleepless nights. The fear of being wrong. Remember this: you were not called to please people but to pastor them. Those are not the same thing. Pleasing them may comfort them, but pastoring them will transform them. Their preferences can kill a church. Your responsibility is not to give them what they want, but to lead them where God is calling.

Do not confuse friendship with leadership. Friends avoid conflict; pastors confront it. Friends seek harmony; pastors seek truth. Maintain clear boundaries between the two. Pray before every major decision. Fast if needed. Wait for God's direction before acting. Involve key leaders early, not to get permission, but to gain perspective and help the congregation see the wisdom of the decision. When respected voices support a difficult choice, opposition often softens. But once

God gives clarity, stand firm. Do not waver even when criticism comes. Do not apologize for obedience.

Your goal is not to be remembered as a pastor who kept everyone happy. That is impossible. Your goal is to be remembered as a leader who stood on principle, faith, and mission. Some may leave angry. Some may never understand. But those who remain will grow to respect your integrity. And most importantly, God will honor it. Hard decisions rarely make you popular, but they make you faithful. Popularity fades. Faithfulness endures. It is far better to hear, "Well done, good and faithful servant," than to receive the applause of people whose praise will soon be forgotten.

CHAPTER 13

Always Have Multiple Plans for Logistics

We had spent thousands of dollars spreading the gospel and inviting the community to our evangelistic series. Advertisements. Flyers. Radio spots. Personal invitations. By the first week, we were gaining momentum. People were coming. Decisions were being made. Then, as the second week began, everything changed. The forecast shifted. A thunderstorm was rolling in. In the Mississippi Delta, where I was pastoring, a storm was never a small matter. Our parking lot flooded whenever it rained. It was not paved, and on that flat land, water sat for days without draining. Puddles became ponds. Grass became mud. Cars got stuck. Elderly members could not walk through it. If rain fell before service, parking was almost impossible. That evening, we realized we had a crisis. We were unable to hold a regular service. People would not come if they could not park, and visitors would not return if their first experience was marked by trudging through mud. We had one shot to get this right.

Canceling was not an option. Souls were on the line. People were making decisions. We had to pivot quickly. Since we were already streaming, we ensured the program was available online for those who could not travel. That covered some, but not all. Many could not access the internet, and others longed for the live experience. We could not abandon them. Someone remembered a nearby closed supermarket with a large parking lot. Paved. Dry. Empty. We reached out to the owner, received permission, and mobilized the team. We ran shuttles to and from the church, called every member with a van, organized drivers, and created a schedule within hours. Our Bible instructors spread the word. We called members individually, posted on social media, and made radio announcements. We even secured police presence for safety at the temporary parking area, so people knew where to go and that it was safe. Despite the storm and all the complications that night, we had a strong turnout. People showed up. The program went forward. Decisions were made. Crisis averted.

As the series drew to a close, another severe storm arrived on the final Sabbath, the day of the closing ceremony and baptism. The weather advisory was clear—severe thunderstorm warning. Stay home. Do not travel. We canceled the morning service. We had no choice. The storm was too dangerous. Yet we refused to lose momentum or give up on the baptisms. We pivoted again, the same principle with a different solution. We streamed a powerful sermon from an earlier service to keep people engaged. Then we watched the radar and waited for a window. When the skies cleared by afternoon, we seized the moment. We rescheduled the closing ceremony for 6 p.m. and announced it to everyone by phone and online. That gave people time to prepare. We had no musicians that evening. Our regular pianist was unable to make it on short notice. So we adapted. We used recordings from earlier nights for congregational singing, and an elder who could play filled the gaps during the offering, special music, and the baptismal service. It was not perfect, but it worked. By the end of the service, eighteen people were baptized. Eighteen souls. Two major storms. A flooded parking lot. Sudden changes. What could have derailed the series became a significant victory, not because of perfect planning, but because of flexibility, backup options, and a refusal to quit.

The Lesson

Never rely on a single plan. If you have only one plan, you have no plan at all. You have a wish. Consider likely scenarios and prepare multiple options. It is better to have alternatives you never use than to be stranded when the unexpected happens. The unexpected will happen. Technology will fail. People will cancel. The weather will change. Plans will fall apart. The question is not if, but when. Planning is not only about anticipating success. It is about preparing for disruption, obstacles, and spiritual opposition. Your logistics must be ready. In ministry, your ability to pivot often determines your success. Not your education. Not your preaching ability. Your flexibility, your willingness to adapt, and your capacity to think on your feet when everything goes wrong are what separate effective ministry from failed ministry.

A Biblical Reflection

Paul reminded Timothy, "Study to show yourself approved unto God, a workman who does not need to be ashamed, rightly dividing the word of truth" (2 Timothy 2:15). Preparation comes before the test. You do not prepare during the crisis. You prepare before the crisis, so you are ready when it arrives. This applies to logistics as surely as it does to doctrine. God often entrusts us with people who are fragile, skeptical, or searching for answers. Some will give the church one chance. A first impression can be a lasting one. People often test whether God is real by whether His people are prepared. Poor logistics can become a stumbling block to faith. When people arrive at our churches or evangelistic meetings, they should see passion and preparation, anointing and organization, zeal and planning. Excellence honors God. Sloppiness dishonors Him. Even when things go wrong, people should know that we anticipated problems and prepared solutions.

Jesus modeled readiness. In Matthew 10, when He sent out the twelve, He did not send them with a smile and a blessing alone. He warned them of rejection, persecution, and hardship before they faced it. He prepared them for the worst so they would not be blindsided. Noah built the ark long before the first drop of rain. People mocked the preparation for what they could not see. Joseph stored grain long before the famine. Seven years of preparation for seven years of crisis. Both were called foolish. Both saved nations. Preparation is not a lack of faith. It is faith in action. Faith looks to the God who sees the end from the beginning and chooses to act wisely in the present. Faith prepares. Presumption does not.

Encouragement for New Pastors

If you are starting in ministry, learn early that good intentions are not enough. Passion without planning produces chaos. Vision without backup plans often leads to a crisis. Hope for the best, pray for the best, and expect the best, but prepare for the worst. Build backup plans. Think through scenarios. Ask what could go wrong, then prepare for those things. Plan for sunshine and prepare for rain. Have indoor options for outdoor events. Have technology backups for digital presentations. Line up substitute speakers. Create transportation alternatives when roads flood. Think ahead, prepare alternatives, then trust God with the results.

Do not be discouraged when your first plan collapses. It will happen. Flexibility is not failure. It is wisdom. It is leadership. It is faith expressed through prudence. Some of your most significant victories will come when Plan A crumbles and God meets you in Plan B or Plan C. Repeatedly, the backup proves better than the original. Disruption creates an opportunity you would not have had otherwise. God works through our flexibility. The same God who told Moses to stretch out his rod had already prepared the wind to part the sea. Moses was unaware of the wind. He obeyed. The same God who sent Elijah to the brook had already commanded ravens to feed him there. Elijah was unaware of the ravens. He went. When one resource dried up, another was waiting in the wings. The brook ended, and a widow was prepared. The flour waned, God multiplied it. One door closed, another opened. That is the pattern of God. He always has another plan.

Build a team that can pivot with you. Do not only train people to follow scripts. Train them to think clearly under pressure by role-playing scenarios and practicing pivots. Create a culture where flexibility is expected, not feared. When your team knows how to adapt, you can handle almost anything. Teach them that disruptions are not disasters. They are moments to witness God at work in unexpected ways. Every obstacle is an opportunity for testimony.

Never forget this. It is better to have options you don't need than to need options you don't have. Prepare thoroughly. Plan redundantly. Create backups for your backups. And when your careful plans collapse, because they will at times, do not panic. Do not spiral. Do not quit. Lift your eyes to the hills, for your help still comes from the Lord. He is the Master of the backup plan. Trust Him. Stay flexible. Keep moving forward.

CHAPTER 14

Most Members Will Not Participate

The minority will do the majority. This is one of the hardest truths in ministry. The minority of your church will do most of the work, not because the majority is wicked, but because most people never engage. This pattern is evident in every area of church life, including worship, service, and leadership, but it is most visible in evangelism. The Great Commission becomes the Great Omission for many believers.

I once led a two-week district-wide meeting involving all four churches. We planned for months, trained volunteers, and built excitement. I shared a simple goal: if each member reached three people, we could fill the building. If each family invited their neighbors, we could transform the community. The math was sound, the vision straightforward. But when I shared it, many laughed. Not nervously. Dismissively. They were not laughing because the plan was impossible, but because they had no interest in trying. That laughter revealed their hearts.

When the campaign began, I discovered the depth of the problem. We organized a day to distribute invitation packages throughout our four church territories. The date had been set weeks ahead, with multiple reminders about its importance. Out of more than one hundred members, only six showed up. Six. Many who were once active stopped answering calls or attending meetings as soon as the topic of evangelism came up. They enjoyed social gatherings and Bible studies, but mention evangelism and they vanished.

Most members believe evangelism is the pastor's job. They hired you. They think their tithe pays your salary. They expect you to do the outreach. If they help, they act as if they are doing you a favor rather than fulfilling their own mission as disciples. That is the mindset. Evangelism requires effort, sacrifice, and courage. It demands leaving comfort zones, risking rejection, and learning new skills. Many are not willing to pay that cost.

However, disinterest is not the only reason people fail to participate. Many are genuinely afraid because they have never received proper training. They fear rejection, ridicule, or difficult questions they cannot answer. They feel unqualified to teach Bible studies, knock on doors, or invite neighbors. Fear paralyzes them. These members are not rebellious; they are unprepared. Training removes fear. Mentorship builds confidence. Teaching dispels ignorance. Modeling shows them what is possible. Walking with them step by step builds courage. Start in the classroom, move to observation, then to participation, and finally to independence. This process transforms fearful members into confident witnesses.

Some will never engage, even after training. Accept that reality and refuse to let it discourage you. Pour into the willing. Train the timid. Leave the unwilling to God.

The Lesson

Only a small portion of your church will engage in evangelism, typically between ten and twenty percent, and sometimes less. That is not a failure of leadership or preaching. It reflects human nature. Jesus Himself did not get all His followers to evangelize. A few carried the early church while the rest watched. You cannot allow discouragement to stop you. Accept this truth, grieve it if you must, and move on. Work with those who are ready. Train those who are hesitant. You cannot make people care about souls.

A Biblical Reflection

Throughout Scripture, God consistently used small groups of faithful people to accomplish His purpose. Gideon began with thirty-two thousand soldiers, but God reduced them to three hundred so that Israel would know victory came from Him (Judges 7). Moses and Aaron stood before Pharaoh, two men against an empire, yet God used them to free millions. Jesus began His movement with twelve disciples, and even one of them betrayed Him. If Jesus did not get full participation from His handpicked team, why should you expect to?

God does not need large numbers. He values faithfulness over size, quality over quantity, and commitment over enthusiasm. That faithfulness grows through intentional preparation. Jesus spent three years teaching, mentoring, and modeling before sending His disciples out. They watched Him minister to the woman at the well, to Nicodemus, to tax collectors, and to sinners. Only after that training did He commission them to go. The same pattern applies today: teach, model, and then send. Do not expect people to do what they have never seen you do.

Encouragement for New Pastors

If you are a new pastor, the disinterest of others will test you. It will hurt when you announce evangelism training and three people show up. You will question your leadership when no one volunteers. That pain is normal. Feel it, then keep going. Begin with those who are willing, even if they are not your elders or officers. It might be the young single mother, the new believer, or the quiet member in the back pew. Often, the overlooked are the most ready to serve.

Invest your best energy into them. Train them well. Set clear, measurable goals and celebrate small victories. Sometimes you and your family will be the only ones willing to work. Start there. God honors small beginnings. Start with three, and in six months you may have seven. A year later, fifteen. New believers are the most evangelistic because they still remember what it means to be lost. As you disciple them, they will build the culture of evangelism your church needs. Over time, evangelism will become the norm, not the exception.

Do not waste time complaining about those who refuse to help. Do not shame them in sermons or gossip about them in private. Some people will debate church budgets or carpet colors for hours, but vanish when it is time to reach souls. It has always been this way. Do not let it embitter you. Focus on the willing and the timid, not the unwilling.

When you put your hand to the plow, God will provide the increase. Faithfulness is not measured by numbers but by obedience. You are not responsible for results, only for faithfulness. God used Gideon's three hundred to defeat an army, Moses' staff to part the sea, and eleven disciples to change the world. He can also use your few faithful members. Train them, mentor them, and watch Him turn their fear into boldness. Start with the few. God will multiply.

CHAPTER 15

Pastoring by God's Direction

The easiest place to make enemies is the church. The fastest way to make them is to become a pastor. You can make enemies by doing the wrong thing, but what surprised me most is that you can also make enemies by doing the right thing, especially by doing the right thing. I learned this lesson early in ministry.

Before I was installed in my first district, before preaching a single sermon, a member obtained my number and sent me a detailed list of her expectations for me as her pastor. It was not a suggestion. It was a numbered list. She had typed it, printed it, and mailed it as though it were a contract. She explained how the previous pastor had let her down. He did not visit enough. He did not preach her favorite topics. He did not run the church the way she thought he should. She demanded that I meet all her expectations immediately.

I respectfully told her that I would not accept a personal to-do list. I was not her employee. I was the congregation's pastor. I invited her to share her suggestions at the upcoming constituency meeting, where the entire church could discuss them collectively. That was the proper process, transparent and fair. Later, I learned she had done the same with every pastor before and after me. This was her pattern. Every new pastor received the list, and every pastor who refused it lost her support. She was not seeking a pastor. She wanted a puppet.

That experience taught me something the seminary never mentioned. In ministry, you are usually loved until you say no. The moment you disappoint someone's expectations, you can become their enemy. One disagreement can turn admiration into accusation. You will often be criticized by many and supported by a few, and the criticism will always sound louder than the encouragement. In those moments, I had to remain anchored in God's vision even when misunderstood, criticized, or left standing alone. His approval had to matter more than theirs.

The Lesson

Your ultimate responsibility is to God, not to the expectations of people. Let that truth govern every decision because people will test it daily. You do not work for the church or for the conference. You work with them, but you work for God. The church does not sign your eternal paycheck. God does. The conference does not determine your success. God does. Forget this, and you will become a people pleaser instead of a God pleaser.

He is the one who called you. They may have voted for your employment, but God is the one who hired you. His will must always take precedence over human preference, even when it costs you relationships or comfort. This will sometimes require you to say no to projects that glorify people more than God, to programs that preserve tradition but produce no disciples, and to spending that comforts members while neglecting mission. Saying no is pastoral work.

At other times, you will need to take a stand that brings criticism and conflict. People will accuse you of being divisive, of lacking love, of destroying unity. They may threaten to leave or withhold the tithe. They may speak against you publicly. The consequences will be real. Take the stand anyway. The pastor who fears people more than God cannot lead faithfully. Fear of man enslaves. Fear of God liberates. One brings compromise. The other brings wisdom. You must choose which will rule you.

A Biblical Reflection

The life of Jesus reveals this tension perfectly. In Gethsemane, His humanity recoiled at the suffering ahead. He prayed, "If it is possible, let this cup pass from me." Yet He surrendered, saying, "Not my will, but yours be done" (Matthew 26:39). Redemption came not through pleasing people but through obeying God's will, even when obedience meant loneliness and pain.

We see the same principle when Jesus faced the woman caught in adultery. The crowd expected Him to condemn her according to the law. It was a trap, a test of His allegiance. Instead, He revealed the Father's heart: "Neither do I condemn you. Go and sin no more." That decision cost Him popularity, but it fulfilled His purpose. Scripture is consistent on this point. When God's will and human expectation collide, the faithful servant always chooses God. You cannot serve two masters. When their demands diverge, obedience to God must win.

Encouragement for New Pastors

If you are a new pastor, expect this tension daily. Every decision will test whether you fear God or people. Members will present personal agendas disguised as divine direction. They will say, "This is how we have always done it," or, "You need to respect our culture." Leaders may pressure you to conform to political or traditional norms. Resist the urge to compromise your calling for comfort.

God's voice must remain the loudest voice in your life, louder than your spouse's concerns, your children's needs, your members' opinions, and your own fears. Sometimes He will confirm His will through wise counsel or consensus, but more often He will speak in prayer, through His Word, and by the quiet conviction of the Spirit. You must know His voice. Without it, every complaint will shake you, every threat will intimidate you, and every demand will control you. Intimacy with God is not optional. It is survival.

People will not always agree with you. Most will not. But if you consistently align with God, many will respect you. They may dislike your decisions, but will honor your integrity. Consistency builds credibility. And when even that respect fades, when mockery replaces praise and loyalty turns to betrayal, rest in this assurance. If God is pleased, that is enough. His approval is your anchor when human applause fades. Ask yourself regularly, "Is God pleased with me?" If the answer is yes, stand firm.

Pastoring is not about being everyone's friend. It is about being their shepherd. Shepherds lead. Friends follow. Shepherds protect the flock even when the sheep resist. Friends often avoid conflict to maintain peace. You are not called to please the flock. You are called to guide them. Walk in the anointing of God, not in the expectations of people. His grace will sustain you wherever His will leads. Human approval is temporary. God's approval is eternal. Choose wisely.

PART V – MINISTRY IS MESSY

CHAPTER 16

Youth Are Vulnerable and Require Authenticity

It is often said that young people are the future of the church. I disagree. That statement is a way of excusing their neglect in the present. They are not the future. They are the present. Treating them as a future priority delays the responsibility to nurture, mentor, and empower them now. When you say that youth are the future, what you are really saying is that youth can wait.

When I arrived at my first district, I quickly realized that there were few young people in the churches. Rural Mississippi. Aging congregations. The few youth who attended were disengaged. Not rebellious, just absent. They were physically present on some Sabbaths but emotionally disconnected. There were no programs, no mentorship, no leadership opportunities. They were told to sit quietly and observe while adults handled everything. That was their role: to observe, not to participate.

My wife and I knew something had to change. We had no budget and no volunteers, but we could not ignore them. We started simple youth programs every Sabbath afternoon. Nothing elaborate. We played games, shared Scripture, and most importantly, talked with them. Not lecturing, not preaching, but really listening to their stories, their thoughts, and their struggles. Those conversations shattered my assumptions. Young people are not disinterested in God. They are open, searching, and asking deep questions. They crave authenticity, not performance.

The idea that young people are disinterested in church often stems from adults who fail to take the time to get to know them. Adults project their assumptions: "They only want entertainment." "They're addicted to their phones." "They don't care about spiritual things." These assumptions are often false, based on distant observation rather than personal experience or relationship. It is not that they dislike God. They are hungry for God but turned off by hypocrisy. They see adults say one thing on Sabbaths and live another way during the week. They hear sermons about love but watch gossip and division. They are told to be honest, yet they see dishonesty among leaders. That disconnect drives them away. What they want is genuine faith. Real people with real struggles who have a real relationship with a real God. They enjoy belonging, not just being a member. A safe place where they can question without being condemned and doubt without being dismissed.

One of the most valuable lessons I learned was to ask more questions than I gave answers. As pastors, we are trained to provide solutions, but young people open up when you ask instead of preach. When you ask, they share. When you listen, they talk. When you judge, they hide. When you accept, they reveal. I heard stories of abuse, addiction, depression, doubt, failure, and rejection. And in those honest moments, I learned that some of the insights I sought as a pastor were already within them. They see things we often miss. They understand culture more than we do. They have the wisdom we need, but they will only share it if they trust us.

Trust takes time. I call it "trust currency," and you earn it through consistency. By showing up. By keeping promises. By maintaining confidentiality. By staying calm when they share something difficult. Over time, the youth in my district came to realize that I was a trustworthy individual. They knew they could speak without being shamed. That trust allowed them to share deeper struggles and opened doors for true ministry. Many of those same youth became the first to come to Christ. Their honesty and vulnerability created a spiritual openness that led to transformation.

The Lesson

Never underestimate the value of youth. They are not optional in ministry. They are essential. Do not treat them as a second priority or give them leftover attention after tending to adults. Do not assume someone else will reach them. They are central to the life and growth of the church. Many of the baptisms I performed were of youth and young adults. Most of the fundamental transformation I witnessed happened among them. They are in a stage where formation and change are possible. Their vulnerability makes them receptive to God. Adults have learned to hide. Youth are still transparent, and that transparency is a gift. Steward it well.

A Biblical Reflection

When the disciples tried to turn children away, believing they were too insignificant to bother Jesus, He rebuked them:

"Let the little children come to me, and do not hinder them, for the kingdom of heaven belongs to such as these" (Matthew 19:14). The kingdom belongs to such as these, not to the religious elite, not to the powerful, but to the open and sincere. Jesus saw value where others saw distraction. He welcomed their honesty and vulnerability.

Throughout Scripture, God repeatedly used young people. Samuel was still a boy when he first heard God's voice. David was a youth when he faced Goliath. Esther was a young woman who risked her life for her people. Timothy was so young that Paul had to remind him, "Do not let anyone look down on you because you are young, but set an example for the believers in speech, in conduct, in love, in faith, in purity" (1 Timothy 4:12). God specializes in using those whom others overlook. Age, experience, or credentials have never limited Him. He looks for faith, not familiarity: availability, not age.

Encouragement for New Pastors

If you are a new pastor, do not let youth ministry intimidate you. You do not need a special degree, a large budget, or elaborate programs. Start with relationships. Programs without relationships accomplish little, but relationships without programs can still bear fruit. Before planning events or purchasing materials, sit down with your youth to discuss their needs and interests. One on one. In small groups. Listen to them. Let them share with you where they are spiritually and what they yearn for.

Do not assume you know what they need. You grew up in a different time, with different challenges. Let them teach you about their world. Ask them. Believe what they tell you. They are searching for authenticity more than entertainment. They are wrestling with issues of identity, purpose, and faith that the church often avoids. When they are not in church, they are not always at parties. Usually, they are alone, scrolling, watching, searching for meaning. The internet will shape them if the church does not. That is why your presence matters. You are not just offering youth ministry. You are competing for their souls.

Reflect on your own experiences as a young person. The loneliness. The unanswered questions. The doubts you buried. The times you felt invisible. Think of what you wish your pastor had done for you, and do that for them. Be honest about your struggles and transparent about your faith journey. They do not need a perfect pastor. They need a real one.

Above all, remember that relationships are the foundation of effective ministry. Everything else is secondary. Young people want to be seen, heard, and loved. If you can offer them that, without judgment and without an agenda, you will not only keep them in church but also help them encounter the living Christ.

CHAPTER 17

Adjusting to Different Cultures in Ministry

Culture will either make or break your ministry. Understand it, and it becomes a bridge to people's hearts. Ignore it, and it becomes a wall you will never cross. Ministry never happens in isolation. It takes place within the realities of people's lives, which are shaped by culture; their history, pain, celebrations, unspoken rules, and collective memory. Culture is the water they swim in. If you do not understand that water, you will drown trying to reach them.

I was born and raised in Jamaica, a country with one of the highest concentrations of Seventh-day Adventists worldwide. There, being an Adventist is normal, even expected. Adventism is deeply embedded in the nation's culture. Businesses accommodate Sabbath-keepers. Government officials are often Adventists. The society supports the faith. When I moved to New York, I entered a different world. The city was a vibrant mosaic of cultures, comprising influences from the Caribbean, Africa, Asia, Europe, and Latin America. You could travel the world without leaving the city. Later, when I lived in Boston, that diversity deepened my appreciation for the varied nature of ministry. I learned that what succeeds in one culture can fail in another. Worship styles differ. Communication patterns vary. Authority structures shift. I thought I understood cross-cultural ministry until I moved to Mississippi.

In Mississippi, the reality was entirely different. Culture shock was immediate. The South was far less diverse. The region where I served was shaped almost entirely by two groups: African American and Caucasian. Their shared history and tension defined much of their lives. Even within the Adventist churches, I discovered a very different culture from what I had been accustomed to. Worship was more relaxed. Services started later. The dress was less formal. Traditions reflected the influence of Baptist, Pentecostal, and Church of God in Christ practices. Call and response. Testimonies. Extended singing. Emotional expression. This was not the formal Adventism of my upbringing. My preaching felt too structured. My tone felt too rigid. My expectations felt foreign. What worked in Jamaica or New York did not work here. I had to adapt.

One of the first adjustments came with funerals. In Jamaica, funerals never occur on the Sabbath. Sabbath is for worship, not mourning. The dead are buried on Sunday. That is the norm, unquestioned. But in Mississippi, Sabbath funerals are common. Expected. Most take place on Sabbath afternoon. At first, I struggled. It felt wrong. It went against everything I knew. I wondered how to participate without compromising conviction. Eventually, I found peace in understanding that, while the practice was unfamiliar, it was not sinful. My role was to show compassion, recognizing that Sabbath is a day for pastoral care, not exclusion. Compassion had to matter more than cultural comfort. Paul's words in Romans reminded me, "Rejoice with those who rejoice, mourn with those who mourn" (Romans 12:15). He did not say to mourn only on culturally acceptable days. Ministry had to be greater than my preferences.

Another adjustment came through pastoral expectations. In Jamaica, pastors are highly visible, constantly leading, visiting, and attending every meeting. Presence equals care. In Mississippi, members valued privacy. Frequent home visits felt intrusive. They preferred their pastor to be available when needed, rather than always present. Their culture valued boundaries. To serve effectively, I had to honor that. I had to learn that respect sometimes meant restraint.

The longer I served, the more I realized that cultural intelligence is not optional. It is essential. Every pastor must develop it. Many of my members had never left the state of Mississippi. Their worldview was local, not global. Church culture passed through families like an inheritance. Without understanding that context, I would never lead effectively. So I listened. I read. I asked questions. I learned the history and pain of the African American experience. Only then could I minister authentically and empathically.

The Lesson

If you cannot respect culture, you will fail as a pastor. You may preach well and have a deep understanding of theology, but without cultural awareness, you will not connect with your congregation. Culture shapes how people see the world. It defines what feels normal or strange, how they relate to authority, whether they trust institutions, and how they express worship. It determines if they are direct or indirect, time-oriented or event-oriented, individualistic or communal. The same applies to church culture. Each congregation has its own rhythm; its own pace, style, and sacred traditions. Violating that rhythm brings resistance, even when change is needed.

A Biblical Reflection

Paul expressed this principle when he said, "I have become all things to all people, so that by all possible means I might save some" (1 Corinthians 9:22). He did not compromise truth. He adapted his approach. The gospel remains the same, but the method must fit the context. Ministry is more effective when we meet people within their cultural reality rather than forcing them into ours. The message remains unchanged, but its presentation must be contextually appropriate.

Jesus modeled this perfectly. He met Nicodemus, a respected Jewish leader, in the quiet of the night because his culture required privacy. He met the Samaritan woman in daylight because her culture required visibility. He healed the servant of a Roman centurion, breaking barriers of ethnicity and class. He touched lepers, ate with tax collectors, and spoke with women in public. Every action was intentional, designed to reveal that the kingdom of God transcends culture. Jesus changed His method but never His message. That is the pattern for cross-cultural ministry.

Adjusting to Different Cultures in Ministry

Encouragement for New Pastors

If you serve in a culture different from your own, take time to learn it. Listen more than you speak. Observe before judging. Assumptions will deceive you. Stereotypes will blind you. Every cultural habit has a story behind it. When you learn the story, you gain understanding and build trust. When you criticize without understanding, you destroy trust that may never be restored.

Do not resist culture unless it directly contradicts the Word of God. Most cultural practices are not sinful; they are simply different. Adapt when possible. Adjust your preaching style, illustrations, and presence to fit the people you serve. Formal or casual. Visible or subtle. Structured or flexible. Ministry requires humility to meet people where they are. When members see that you respect their culture and traditions, they open their hearts. That trust is your greatest resource, more valuable than education or eloquence.

Always remember that faithfulness to God comes first. Culture never outweighs Scripture. When culture and Scripture conflict, Scripture stands. Yet such conflicts are rare. Most differences are stylistic, not spiritual. Within the wide boundaries of God's will, cultural awareness strengthens your ministry. It builds trust, removes barriers, and allows the gospel to be heard without offense. When your members see that you not only preach among them but live with them, eat their food, honor their history, and share their joys and sorrows, hearts open. Barriers fall. Change begins. All because you took the time to understand their culture.

CHAPTER 18

Some People Love Conflict and Do Not Desire Peace

Some people love conflict. This is one of the hardest truths in ministry to accept. They wake up looking for it. They create it when it doesn't exist. They seek opportunities to sow confusion in the life of the church. Not because they are addressing real problems, but because conflict itself energizes them. In my district, I quickly realized that some individuals were amicable, kind, supportive, and peaceful. But others seemed driven by conflict.

These are the ones who rarely have anything good to say about anyone else. Their conversations are filled with criticism, negativity, and suspicion. They often begin with phrases like, "I don't mean any harm, but…" which is a warning sign. What follows will always be harmful. Or they say, "Don't tell anyone I told you this, but…" which is another red flag. They are about to gossip.

I learned to watch for the cues. Conflict-driven individuals tend to speak more than they should, dominating conversations, interrupting others, and insisting on the last word. They show up in conversations that do not concern them, attend every meeting, and insert themselves into every discussion. If conflict exists, they are involved. Guaranteed. They always have an opinion, usually negative, about what others are doing. The music is too loud. The sermon is too long. The offering is too frequent. The youth are too casual. Always complaining. They thrive on pointing out problems without offering solutions. Ask them for solutions, and they vanish. Problems energize them; solutions bore them. If left unchecked, they can tear at the fabric of a congregation. Slowly at first, a comment here and a criticism there. Then, it speeds up until divisions form, factions emerge, and unity crumbles. All because one or two people were allowed to operate without accountability.

One experience still makes me angry when I think about it. A church member took in a fellow member who had been abandoned by his family and was suffering from medical issues. She nursed him, cooked his meals, and gave him a home until he eventually passed away. She was grieving the loss of a friend and a church brother. After months of caregiving and watching him decline, she was exhausted, heartbroken, and in need of support from her church family. Instead of surrounding her with compassion, some members seized the opportunity to attack her character. They accused her of living in sin because she shared a home with a man who was not her husband.

Never mind that he was dying. Never mind that she was caring for him. Never mind that there was no evidence of impropriety. They saw an opportunity to create conflict and took it. Their accusations were not based on truth, evidence, witness testimony, or anything resembling reality. Their motive was simple: to stir up trouble and destroy this woman's reputation. To punish her for showing Christlike compassion in a way that made them uncomfortable. The grief-stricken member nearly lashed out physically. I could not blame her.

The accusation was so unjust, so cruel, and so perfectly timed to maximize her pain that anger seemed like the only reasonable response. Thankfully, another sister, guided by pastoral counsel, intervened before the situation escalated.

That incident reminded me that some people overlook humanity in their pursuit of discord. A dying man became a prop for their accusations. A grieving woman became their target. They do not seek peace. They would hate peace, for peace would leave them nothing to do. They seek power through conflict, control through chaos. If left unresolved, such situations fester. What begins as a small sore eventually becomes a wound, then an infection, then gangrene, and finally death. The progression is predictable. You can see it coming if you are willing to act early, while the sore is still small and treatable.

The Lesson

Conflict is unavoidable and guaranteed, but it must never be ignored. When conflict threatens the unity, health, or progress of the congregation, it must be addressed quickly, directly, and biblically. Delay only makes it worse. Pastors must learn to recognize those who thrive on discord and deal with them in a wise manner. Not harshly. Not publicly. But firmly. These individuals will test your boundaries and push to see how much chaos you will tolerate. You must establish early that you will tolerate none.

A Biblical Reflection

The Bible provides clear guidance on handling conflict. Jesus outlined a process in Matthew 18:15–17. First, approach the individual privately, one-on-one, without an audience or public shaming. If that fails, bring one or two others to witness the conversation for accountability and clarity. If it remains unresolved, take it before the church. Public discipline is for public problems. This model is practical and Spirit-led. It emphasizes both accountability and restoration. You are not trying to destroy the person but to restore them. Restoration requires accountability. Accountability without restoration becomes punishment. Restoration without accountability becomes enabling. You need both.

Paul also warned that "God is not the author of confusion but of peace" (1 Corinthians 14:33). Wherever confusion reigns and chaos dominates, God is not the source. God brings peace; the enemy brings disorder. When your church is constantly in turmoil, spiritual warfare is taking place. Pastors must therefore stand firmly on biblical principles when addressing conflict, not on personal preferences or traditions. Guide both the offender and the offended with love and compassion. Both need your care. The offender needs correction, and the offended needs protection. Your role is to provide both.

Encouragement for New Pastors

If you are new in ministry, expect conflict. Not if it comes, but when. Not occasional conflict, but continual strife. Do not be caught off guard. Prepare yourself mentally and spiritually for the challenges that lie ahead. Wherever people gather, disagreements will occur. Church is no exception. We are not holier; we are forgiven. Some will stir conflict because they are hurting. Wounded people wound others. Some will stir it because they crave control. Either way, you must address it. Ignoring it does not make it disappear; it makes it multiply.

Do not take sides. Members will pressure you to choose. Resist it. Stand on the side of Scripture. Always. Confront the issue without attacking the person's dignity. Correct firmly but love sincerely. Firm correction shows you care about the truth. Sincere love shows you care about people. Both matter. If conflict is left unresolved, it will grow. One conflict becomes two; two become four; soon, the church is divided. However, when conflict is handled wisely, addressed promptly, and guided by Scripture, it can produce unity and trust. When members see that you will not tolerate chaos, they feel safe, and unity strengthens.

Above all, guard your spirit. Conflict can drain you, exhaust you, and make you bitter, cynical, or resentful. Do not carry it alone. It will crush you. Lean on trusted pastors who have wisdom, mentors who have walked similar roads, and your spouse, if married, who sees the toll conflict takes on you. Pray for the Spirit to give you discernment, to show you what is happening beneath the surface, and to give wisdom for when to engage and when to wait. Remind yourself daily that your calling is to shepherd God's people toward peace. Some will never desire peace. Some will actively resist it. Some will sabotage every attempt. Your job is not to force peace. Your job is to lead toward it. Some will follow. Some will not. Lead anyway.

CHAPTER 19

Dealing with Gossip

Church folk love to gossip. This should not surprise us, but somehow it always does. One of the unavoidable realities of pastoral ministry is the prevalence of gossip. Not occasional gossip, but constant gossip. Many church members engage in it without realizing the harm their words cause. Others know it is destructive yet continue anyway. Some even convince themselves that spreading rumors is a moral duty. They call it concern. They call it accountability. They call it keeping the pastor informed. It is gossip dressed in spiritual language.

The rumor mill operates without verification, investigation, or confirmation. Stories are repeated and reshaped as they pass from person to person. By the time you hear them, they have been told ten times and edited ten different ways. What begins as a whisper soon becomes a wildfire, uncontrollable and consuming everything in its path.

When I first became pastor of my district, the earliest gossip about my wife and me was that we were not converted Christians. This started before I preached my first sermon, before anyone knew us, before we had done anything. The reason? We wore wedding bands. Two pieces of jewelry were said to determine our spiritual state, according to the gossip. Members whispered behind our backs in the parking lot, in the fellowship hall, and on the phone, accusing us of violating church standards. We were labeled worldly, unspiritual, and compromised. Our character was assassinated before we could even introduce ourselves.

Another painful experience came during a youth program. The church was packed with young people, many of whom had not attended in years. The energy was powerful, the worship vibrant, and lives were being touched. Yet before long, people who were not even present began spreading rumors that the program was immoral and ungodly. They did not see the worship. They did not witness the altar calls. They did not experience the Spirit's movement. But they had opinions, strong ones. Instead of celebrating what God was doing, they chose to criticize from a distance.

Moments like these raise difficult questions that every pastor wrestles with. Can I trust my members? Can I lean on them when I am overwhelmed? Or will vulnerability be weaponized? Can I be transparent without my words being twisted? Can I share struggles without them becoming sermon illustrations in gossip sessions? Gossip erodes a pastor's confidence slowly but surely. It leaves pastors feeling unsupported, exposed, and at times betrayed by their own flock. The people you are called to shepherd can become the source of your deepest wounds. That is a unique kind of pain.

The Lesson

Gossip in ministry is unavoidable. You will be gossiped about. Count on it. But remember this: it is not always about you. In fact, it usually is not. Gossip says more about the character of those who spread it than the one being spoken about. It reveals insecurity, jealousy, and a hunger for control. It exposes spiritual immaturity. Gossip damages morale, divides members, and weakens focus on mission. It turns energy that should be spent on evangelism into energy wasted on infighting. It also tarnishes the church's reputation in the community. Outsiders hear how Christians talk about each other and wonder, "If that is how they treat their own, why would I join them?"

Gossip is poison. It kills evangelism, weakens unity, and destroys credibility. It spares no one: neither the speaker, nor the target, nor the listener.

A Biblical Reflection

Scripture repeatedly warns about the power of the tongue. James calls it "a world of evil among the parts of the body; it corrupts the whole person" (James 3:6). Gossip does not merely harm others; it corrupts the gossiper. Proverbs declares, "Life and death are in the power of the tongue" (Proverbs 18:21). Words are never neutral. They either build or destroy. Gossip, left unchecked, spreads like a vine, growing quickly and bearing poisonous fruit.

But the Bible also teaches how to respond. Paul counsels, "Let your conversation be always full of grace, seasoned with salt, so that you may know how to answer everyone" (Colossians 4:6). Grace, not gossip. Salt, not poison. This must be the standard for Christian speech. When you hear gossip, and you will, your response must be shaped by grace, not anger or revenge. Do not fight gossip with gossip. Do not match their tone. Do not sink to their level. When you are tempted to speak about others, stop and ask yourself: Is what I'm about to say true? Is it kind? Is it necessary? If the answer to any of these is no, remain silent. Let your words bring healing, not harm. Let them build bridges, not walls.

Encouragement for New Pastors

If you are wounded by gossip, and you will be, know that you are not alone. Every pastor has walked this road. The pain is real and deep. Church wounds cut differently from those of the world. Gossip should not exist in ministry, but it does. Even redeemed people gossip. Even Spirit-filled people fail. Sin dies slowly, and gossip is one of the last sins to surrender.

If gossip angers or isolates you, acknowledge those emotions. Do not bury them. If the gossip is severe enough to damage your credibility or relationships, follow the steps outlined in Matthew 18. Go directly to the person. Not to a crowd. Speak calmly and privately. Address the issue with dignity. Never respond to gossip with gossip. Do not defend yourself by attacking others. Be the place where gossip ends, not where it spreads.

Rise above it by staying faithful to your calling. Keep preaching. Keep shepherding. Keep loving. If correction is needed, make it brief, clear, and gracious. Then move forward. If the situation cannot be corrected without causing more harm, let your faithfulness be your defense. Time and consistency will silence falsehood. Gossip can delay your progress, but it cannot stop what God has ordained.

Remember: a gossiping church is never a missional church. When members are busy spreading rumors, they have no energy left for sharing the gospel. The time that should be spent in prayer or service is wasted in conversation. As the old saying goes, Satan always finds work for idle hands. Gossip is his favorite occupation for Christians who have forgotten their mission.

Guard your spirit. Surround yourself with people who speak truth and encouragement. Find those who remind you of God's promises when gossip clouds your heart. Their words will anchor you when others' words wound you.

Gossip may hurt you, but it cannot cancel what God has confirmed. Shepherd faithfully. Keep your eyes on Christ, who endured slander, lies, and mockery. They called Him demon-possessed. They called Him insane. They accused Him of blasphemy. Yet He remained faithful. If He endured with grace, so can you, through His Spirit.

CHAPTER 20

Extending Grace When People Lack Integrity

Not everyone will deal with you honorably. This is one of the most challenging realities of ministry. People you trust will lie about you. People you serve will misrepresent you. People you pour into will betray you. It is not a matter of if but when. At some point, likely more than once, you will face individuals who lie about you or twist your intentions. Blatantly. Deliberately. To your face or behind your back.

It is excruciating because, as a pastor, you give so much of yourself. Your time, prayers, energy, heart, your family's time, and even your marriage's strength all become sacrifices for ministry. Yet despite all that, there will be moments when people take what you said and make it mean something entirely different. They will misrepresent your actions, assign motives you never had, or create stories that never happened.

I recall one situation where a member called urgently, asking for financial help. Her car had broken down, and she wanted a loan from the church. I explained that the church is not a bank and cannot provide loans. However, I told her that we had a benevolent fund and could raise a love offering to help with her expenses, with no expectation of repayment. I made it clear that the church was willing and ready to assist her. She refused the offer, saying she did not want a gift, only a loan. Perhaps it was pride. Perhaps something else. I reminded her that the door was open and that we were still ready to help if she changed her mind.

Soon after, she stopped coming to church. She blocked my number and ignored my messages—total silence. Eventually, through our mentorship program, I learned that she had told others I had refused to help her. According to her story, she reached out to her pastor in her time of need, and I turned her away coldly and without compassion. That was the version she spread. It was a complete fabrication, but it spread through the mentorship group, through the church, and possibly through the community. Once a lie starts spreading, it is almost impossible to stop.

What made this hurt even more was remembering how I had driven over an hour each way to visit her in the hospital several times. I had prayed with her, encouraged her, stayed by her side, brought her communion, and checked on her regularly. I had gone above and beyond. And this was how she repaid that investment. The same person I had supported now accused me of being cold and unhelpful. It felt like betrayal. It was betrayal.

The Lesson

This experience taught me that as a pastor, I am held to a higher standard, whether I like it or not. Whether it feels fair or not. I cannot stoop to the level of deceit or retaliation, even when others abandon integrity. Even when defending myself would be easy. Even when retaliation would feel justified, I must maintain integrity when others forsake it.

I must hold my character steady and extend grace, even when it feels undeserved, especially when it seems unwarranted. Grace toward the deserving is not grace; it is a transaction. True grace is what you extend to those who least deserve it. That is when it costs something.

A Biblical Reflection

The life of Jesus offers the clearest model for handling dishonesty. When He stood before the Sanhedrin, false witnesses accused Him of things He never said or did. Lies. Complete fabrications. Yet He did not retaliate with anger. He did not defend Himself or correct every falsehood. He remained silent and committed Himself to the Father who judges righteously (1 Peter 2:23). His silence was not weakness but strength. It was not an inability to respond but a refusal to respond. Jesus understood what we often forget: God's defense is better than our defense. Always.

Romans 12:17–21 reinforces this truth: "Do not repay anyone evil for evil. If it is possible, as far as it depends on you, live at peace with everyone. Do not be overcome by evil, but overcome evil with good." The phrase "as far as it depends on you" carries weight. You cannot control their response; you can only control yours. Do your part and trust God with theirs. This principle anchors us in ministry. When people lie about you or misrepresent your intentions, your response must be grace, not retaliation or bitterness. Do not gossip about them. Trust God to defend you. His defense is better than yours, and His timing is perfect. God can use their lies to refine your character, their betrayal to strengthen your faith, and their dishonesty to reveal His faithfulness.

Encouragement for New Pastors

If you are dealing with dishonesty in your ministry and the pain is still fresh, know that you are not alone. Every pastor faces this. Most face it many times. It is part of the cost of pastoral ministry. That does not make it hurt less, but it reminds you that you are not being singled out. The temptation will be to defend yourself harshly, to call people out publicly, to retaliate, or to withdraw in frustration. You may even consider quitting. Those temptations are natural, but resist them. Protect your heart. Bitterness will destroy you faster than any lie will.

Speak the truth. Lies left unchallenged can become an accepted norm. But tell the truth in a way that does not destroy. Correct the falsehood without destroying the person who spread it. Address the behavior without attacking their dignity. Always leave room for reconciliation. Do not burn bridges you may later need to cross.

Guard your leadership by ensuring that your side of the story is told truthfully and with grace—document where necessary. Keep witnesses when appropriate. Tell the truth without vindictiveness. Correct lies without cruelty. Your integrity in response matters more than their integrity in accusation. Do not let lies define you, but do not let them make you bitter either. Bitterness is like drinking poison and expecting the other person to die. They will not. You will.

Your calling is not to protect your reputation but to reflect Christ. He was lied about, betrayed, and falsely accused. If it happened to Him, it will happen to you. He warned you: "If they persecuted Me, they will persecute you" (John 15:20). That includes lies.

Extend grace, even when it is undeserved. This does not mean ignoring dishonesty or failing to set boundaries. Protect yourself. Grace does not mean becoming a doormat or pretending nothing happened. It means recognizing that the one who wronged you is still someone God wants to redeem. You can hold them accountable and still treat them with dignity. Accountability and dignity are not opposites. They belong together.

Finding that balance is difficult. Most pastors wrestle with it their entire lives. Grace without boundaries enables sin. Boundaries without grace harden the heart. The daily work of pastoral leadership involves holding both. Jesus embodied that balance perfectly; we strive toward it daily.

If you can remain faithful in moments of dishonor, if you can keep your integrity when others lie, and maintain your character when others abandon theirs, you will not only preserve your ministry but also teach your congregation what integrity looks like in action. They are watching. How you respond to dishonesty will teach them more than any sermon on integrity. Grace is not weakness. It is the strength to choose character over retaliation.

PART VI – GROWING PAINS

CHAPTER 21

Some People are Untrainable

There is an old Jamaican saying: "You can take the horse to the water, but you cannot make the horse drink." My mother said it often when someone stubbornly refused help. That proverb captures one of the hardest lessons of ministry. As a pastor, you can create opportunities for training, mentorship, teaching, encouragement, and constant support. But growth only happens when a person is willing. Not capable, but willing. You cannot force anyone to grow. You can only create the environment for growth and invite them into it. There are some things you cannot do for people.

When I entered ministry, I was determined to train and develop leaders. I wanted to pour into others, not only by providing them with documents and policies, but also through one-on-one mentorship, deep dialogue, role-playing, practical scenarios, and case studies drawn from real ministry life. I was ready to give my time, knowledge, and experience. I believed that would be enough. Through training and collaboration, leaders can be sharpened, teams can grow, and together we can advance the mission.

However, I soon learned that not everyone wants to grow. Some people are not untrainable because they lack ability or intelligence, but because they lack humility. They are comfortable in their incompetence.

One elder in particular was bright, experienced, and capable, but his pride made him unteachable. He knew better than everyone else. He had been doing this for decades and saw no reason to learn from a younger pastor. When I offered to train him on preaching, covering structure, delivery, and application, he refused, saying he preferred to "do his own thing." The result was painful. When he stood to preach, he embarrassed himself publicly. It was preventable. Completely preventable. He only needed to be willing.

Another example came during an evangelistic series. I asked this same elder to assist with baptisms and made sure to ask beforehand, "Do you know how to perform a baptism correctly?" He assured me that he did. "Of course, Pastor. I have been doing this for years." Yet when the moment came, it was clear he did not. He positioned the candidate dangerously. His method risked injury or worse. His refusal to accept training nearly turned a sacred moment into a tragedy.

When I spoke with him afterward, his resistance was obvious. It was pride. Age-based pride. He could not stand the thought of being corrected by someone younger. He equated tenure with competence, as if years automatically meant growth. They do not.

The Lesson

What I learned from these experiences is simple: you can only train people as much as they are willing to be trained. Not as much as they need to be trained. Not as much as you want to train them. As much as they are willing. Willingness determines growth. Always.

Training cannot be forced. You can require attendance, but you cannot require learning. Growth requires humility from the trainee: "I don't know everything. I am willing to learn." And patience from the trainer: "I will teach this again, and again, until they get it or until they refuse." Both are essential. Neither is enough alone.

A person who is unwilling to be trained is not ready to serve. Placing them in leadership risks the mission. It results in failed programs, embarrassing moments, and weak witnesses. Visitors do not return. Members lose confidence. The unchurched mock. All because someone was too proud to learn.

Willingness is the only doorway to growth. You cannot climb through a window or break down a wall. You must walk through the door. And if the door is closed, you wait—or you find someone whose door is open.

A Biblical Reflection

The Bible affirms this truth throughout. Paul writes in 2 Corinthians 9:7, "Each of you should give what you have decided in your heart to give, not reluctantly or under compulsion." The principle applies beyond giving. Spiritual growth must be voluntary. Willingness is a condition for transformation.

1st Chronicles 28:9 teaches that God desires His servants to serve Him "with wholehearted devotion and with a willing mind." Not halfhearted. Not reluctant. Wholehearted and willing. God does not want coerced service. He wants surrendered hearts. Colossians 3:23–24 echoes the same principle: "Whatever you do, work at it with all your heart, as working for the Lord." Service that pleases God flows from willingness, not pressure.

The story of Apollos in Acts 18 demonstrates this beautifully. Apollos was eloquent, educated, and powerful in Scripture, yet when Priscilla and Aquila took him aside to explain "the way of God more accurately," he listened. He was teachable. His humility allowed him to become one of the great preachers of the early church. His example reminds us that giftedness without humility limits growth, but humility unlocks greater usefulness in God's service.

Encouragement for New Pastors

For new pastors, this truth is both sobering and freeing. Sobering, because not everyone in your congregation will be ready for training. Many will not. Some never will. You will want to help everyone, but you cannot. Some will resist out of pride, tradition, or fear. Freeing, because it reminds you that your job is not to force growth. That belongs to God. Your role is to provide growth opportunities, create the space, offer the tools, and model the process. Their willingness decides the outcome.

When you meet resistance, create safe spaces for reflection. Allow people to see their own limitations. Ask questions rather than lecture. "How do you think that went?" "What might you do differently?" Self-discovery produces change more effectively than public correction. Harsh rebuke creates resentment. Gentle guidance fosters growth.

At the same time, never place unwilling individuals in roles that could harm the church's mission. Tenure does not equal qualification. Willingness to grow does. Protect your ministry by putting the teachable in positions of influence. Place the humble where they can serve well. Leave the unwilling on the sidelines until their hearts are ready.

Model humility yourself. Admit when you do not know something. Confess when you are wrong. Acknowledge your own need for growth. When your members see that you are teachable, it permits them to be trainable.

Your calling is to equip the saints for ministry (Ephesians 4:12). You can lead them to the water, show them how refreshing it is, and model the benefits of growth, but you cannot make them drink. That choice is theirs. Your task is to create opportunities and a culture that values learning. Their task is to respond with willingness. When willingness meets opportunity, discipleship flourishes. Without it, even the best programs fail.

You can guide the willing, but you cannot train the unwilling.

CHAPTER 22

Struggling with Comparison

Comparison is the tendency to place your life or ministry beside someone else's and measure your worth against theirs. It happens quietly, often without warning. A glance at social media. A report at a workers' meeting. A conversation with a colleague. Suddenly, you are measuring, evaluating, questioning. Comparison is subtle, powerful enough to shift how you see everything, and deadly enough to kill your calling if you allow it. I know because I have lived it. I have compared my preaching with others; his delivery smoother, his illustrations sharper, his altar calls more effective. I have compared the tithe returns of my small district with the larger ones, bringing in half a million dollars each month, while my church could only manage a few hundred. I have compared evangelistic results: they baptized fifty; I baptized five. Even beyond ministry outcomes, I have compared myself in areas far outside my control, my church's location, my members' income levels, and my district's demographics. Things I did not choose. Still comparing.

The triggers were predictable. Sitting in workers' meetings and listening to glowing reports about other pastors would stir questions in my heart. Someone was consistently achieving something extraordinary. And I would sit there asking, "What am I doing wrong? Why are their results greater? Why are they celebrated while I am overlooked?" I worked just as hard, maybe harder, yet the outcomes seemed smaller. The more I listened, the more I doubted. The more I doubted, the more I resented my assignment.

Here is the truth I learned the hard way: comparison is a killer. It drains passion until the fire that once burned for ministry goes out. It erodes confidence, causing you to second-guess every decision you make. It steals joy until ministry becomes a matter of survival rather than service. Unchecked, it does not simply weaken your calling; it threatens it entirely.

Why? Because every pastor serves in a different context. Different communities, cultures, resources, and histories. Comparing ministries is like comparing different planets and wondering why they do not look the same. Sin is universal. Grace is universal. However, the scale, challenges, and opportunities vary significantly across the board. One pastor's church has a $100,000 budget, while another has a $10,000 budget. One has a youth pastor; another has three teenagers. One is building a new sanctuary; another is patching a roof. Context changes everything. Comparing your ten-member congregation to a five-hundred-member church is like comparing an apple to an orchard. Nothing is the same except the title "pastor," and even that looks different in every field.

The Lesson

Comparison exposes two dangerous cravings of the heart: insecurity and the longing for approval. We want recognition, validation, and affirmation. And when someone else receives it, comparison whispers, "You are not enough." In chasing someone else's success, we risk abandoning our own calling and imitating a ministry that was never meant to be ours.

Each pastor has been entrusted with a unique, God-designed assignment. You must fight in your own armor, not someone else's. What worked for them may not work for you because God has called you to a different battlefield with different tools. Your context is your armor.

Comparison becomes even more dangerous when it crosses into imitation. Many pastors fall into the trap of mimicking others, copying their gestures, borrowing their phrases, trying to sound like them. They forget that God called them to preach with their own voice. Others go even further, spending money to appear as successful as their peers, buying cars they cannot afford, dressing beyond their means, and enrolling their children in schools they cannot pay for. The desire to look successful leads to debt, stress, and dishonesty. Comparison that begins in the pulpit can end in financial and moral ruin. It can even tempt a pastor to manipulate results or exaggerate numbers to appear effective. Nothing destroys integrity faster.

A Biblical Reflection

The story of David and Goliath captures this principle vividly. When Saul gave David his armor, it seemed like the right thing to do. It was royal armor, proven and prestigious. Yet David quickly realized it was not meant for him. "I cannot go in these," he said, "because I am not used to them" (1 Samuel 17:39). The armor was good, but it was not his. He had to fight with the tools God had given him: his sling, stones, and shepherd's skills.

The same applies to the ministry. We often compare our results to others' visible success without understanding the hidden costs behind them. We see their victories but not their failures, their applause but not their exhaustion, their public success but not their private pain. Many have compromised along the way in ways we cannot see. Ethical shortcuts. Doctrinal concessions. Manipulated outcomes. And yet we compare our honest struggles to their polished appearances.

Scripture reminds us that "each of you should use whatever gift you have received to serve others" (1 Peter 4:10). Whatever gift. Not someone else's. Yours. Paul affirms the same truth in Romans 12:6: "We have different gifts, according to the grace given to each of us." Different does not mean inferior. It means designed for your calling. God has crafted each of us uniquely for the work He has given us to do.

Encouragement for New Pastors

If you are a young pastor wrestling with comparison, pause for a moment and consider this: What is your full name? What is your date of birth? Where do you live? How many people in the world share that exact combination? Only one; you.

Jeremiah 1:5 records God's words: "Before I formed you in the womb I knew you; before you were born I set you apart." Your calling is not random. It is personal. It is particular. Do not measure yourself by another person's assignment. You will either feel inferior or superior, and both will corrupt your spirit. The only accurate measure of success is faithfulness to what God has entrusted to you.

When the temptation to compare rises, and it will, remember that God has given you these people, this place, this moment. Your responsibility is not to copy someone else's results or methods. It is to be faithful with what is in your hands. Faithfulness, not comparison, is the standard of heaven. Comparison distracts, discourages, and derails. Faithfulness centers, strengthens, and sustains.

So, stand firm in your own armor. It fits you. It was made for you. Trust that the God who called you has equipped you with everything necessary to complete your assignment. And never allow the urge to compete to push you into debt or compromise. Do not spend to impress or bend the truth to appear successful. God does not anoint imitation. He anoints authenticity.

Be yourself. That is who He called.

CHAPTER 23

Wait on God's Timing

Stop. Wait. Listen. Trust God's timing, not your timeline or sense of urgency, but His. This is one of the hardest lessons I have learned in ministry. It cost me dearly. I learned it through failure, through watching good plans collapse because I moved too soon. Comparison often tempts us to move faster than God intends. They baptized fifty; I must baptize sixty. They launched three programs; I must launch five. Their church is growing; mine must grow faster. These pressures can push you to act before God says, "Move." You jump when God says, "Stand still."

Every lasting change undergoes a process: prayer, preparation, planning, execution, and evaluation. Each phase requires time. God's timing is measured in seasons, not seconds.

If I could redo my first ninety days of pastoring, I would start differently. I would assess which changes were truly urgent and which could wait. Most could wait. But I did not know that. I saw broken systems, declining ministries, theological confusion, and mission drift—and I wanted to fix it all immediately. My intentions were right, but my timing was wrong. I never stopped to ask the most critical question: Is this God's timing? I asked, "Is it a good idea?" It was. "Does it need to happen?" It did. But I never asked, "Is this the moment?" I learned the answer the hard way.

In an effort to save a struggling congregation, I merged its services with those of a healthier church. Twice a month, one church would close so members could attend the other, hoping to revive the weaker congregation. Our intentions were sincere; we believed no church should die. But despite every sacrifice, the struggling church still closed. I realize now the plan itself was not wrong; it was simply premature. God was ready to close that church, but I was not. My good idea became a bad decision because it was out of season.

Had we focused on strengthening the healthier church first, perhaps growth would have overflowed naturally into the struggling one. Instead, I forced an outcome God had already resolved. It was the right idea at the wrong time. And that made it the wrong move.

The Lesson

Moving before God guarantees failure. You cannot succeed where He has not yet gone ahead of you. When you rely only on logic or urgency, you are applying limited reasoning to divine problems. It will not work. Good intentions are not the same as divine direction. Your sincerity does not compensate for your disobedience.

Without God's timing, even wise plans crumble. The consequences vary: wasted energy, embarrassment, public failure, or months of lost effort. However, the principle remains unchanging: if you move before God, the outcome will not stand.

A Biblical Reflection

Scripture warns us repeatedly against trusting our own understanding. Proverbs 3:5–6 urges, "Trust in the Lord with all your heart and lean not on your own understanding; in all your ways submit to Him, and He will make your paths straight." He directs. You follow. That is the divine order.

Paul reinforces this truth in Galatians 6:9: "Let us not grow weary in doing good, for in due season we shall reap, if we do not lose heart." Not our season; His. "Due season" refers to kairos, God's appointed moment, not chronos, our calendar. God's timing transcends human calculation.

Ecclesiastes reminds us that "there is a season for everything" (3:1). Every event has its appointed season, times to move, times to wait, and times to let go. Disaster strikes when we act during seasons meant for stillness. Running ahead of God is like driving through a red light; you may get through once or twice, but eventually, there will be a collision.

The story of Israel at Ai (Joshua 7) illustrates this clearly. After their victory at Jericho, they assumed success was automatic. Confident in their strategy, they attacked without consulting God. They failed, not due to a lack of effort, but because of misplaced timing. They said, "We're ready," but God had not spoken. Their defeat was inevitable from the outset of the battle. Effort without divine timing always leads to loss.

Encouragement for New Pastors

Do not rush. Do not force outcomes. Slow down. Let things mature at God's pace. His purposes unfold in seasons, not seconds. Patience is not passivity; it is a matter of trust. You see three steps ahead; He sees three hundred. Even when the path appears clear, do not move until you have peace that God has given the green light.

How do you know? Prayer. Scripture. Counsel. Confirmation. Peace. When these align, you can move with confidence.

Cultivate discernment through daily and extended prayer. Ask God not only to show you what to do, but when to do it. The "when" is often as important as the "what." Seek counsel from seasoned pastors who have learned to wait. Their experience can reveal pitfalls that urgency hides. Write your plans down, pray over them, and revisit them after a period of time has passed. What seems urgent today may look foolish tomorrow.

Remember, not every open door is an invitation. Some doors distract. Some appear correct but are premature. And some are traps. The enemy opens doors, too. Open does not mean ordained.

Waiting on God is never wasted time. It is preparation time. Waiting develops character and clarifies motives. Rushing may bring fast results, but they seldom last. Only what is built in God's timing endures.

Trust His timing. You do not have to understand it. You have to obey it. When He opens the right doors in His season, no critic, obstacle, or enemy will be able to close them. What God opens in His time stays open.

PART VII – THE 9 PM PASTOR

CHAPTER 24

Loneliness in Ministry

My understanding of the call to ministry was that it involved challenges in finances, administration, paperwork, meetings, and preaching. What I did not expect, and what nobody warned me about, was how often I would feel alone. Nobody talks about it. It is the silent struggle of pastoral leadership. You can be surrounded by people who need you, yet feel that nobody truly knows you.

There were days when I carried burdens too heavy to share. My members looked to me for strength. They needed stability, not vulnerability. So I stayed silent. My wife was supportive, always steady, but I did not want to overwhelm her with every weight I carried. She had her own adjustments: a new city, a new church, and a new life. To protect her, I shouldered the darkness alone. And with my family far away, there was no natural support system nearby. No parents to visit, no siblings to call, no friends who knew me before I was "Pastor." Even on Sabbaths, surrounded by people, shaking hands, smiling, and preaching, I often felt unseen.

Loneliness in ministry is rarely physical. It is emotional and spiritual. It comes from knowing that some decisions, such as budget, personnel, and conflict, rest on your shoulders alone. The weight of responsibility isolates you. It is the silence that follows the board meeting, when everyone goes home, and you are left questioning whether you made the right call. It is the moment after preaching your heart out, yet having no one to process the emotions with. It is the late-night phone call announcing another crisis, and realizing there is no one else to send. Always you. That constant availability, that unending demand, creates a quiet ache.

The Lesson

Ministry will sometimes feel lonely. That does not mean you are failing or in sin. It means you are human. Leadership requires separation of functions, but not isolation from relationships. You can lead and still have friends. You can be strong and still need support. Loneliness becomes dangerous only when ignored or denied. When you pretend you are fine, it hardens into discouragement, burnout, or moral collapse. Some seek to fill that void through unhealthy means—addiction, emotional entanglements, or overwork. Unaddressed loneliness becomes weaponized against the soul.

A Biblical Reflection

Scripture is full of leaders who knew this struggle. Elijah sat beneath a broom tree, exhausted and convinced he was the only faithful prophet left until God reminded him that seven thousand others had not bowed to Baal (1 Kings 19). His loneliness was real; his isolation was not. Paul wrote letters from prison with only a few companions. Yet, he declared, "The Lord stood with me and strengthened me" (2 Timothy 4:17). Human companionship was limited, but divine presence was constant.

Even Jesus experienced profound aloneness. In Gethsemane, while He agonized in prayer, His disciples slept. On the cross, He cried out, "My God, my God, why have You forsaken me?" (Matthew 27:46). If the sinless Son of God felt alone, we should not be surprised when we do.

Yet none of these stories end in despair. Each shows that God does His deepest work in lonely places. Elijah's silence became the setting for God's whisper. Paul's imprisonment produced letters that still strengthen the church. Jesus' isolation at Calvary brought salvation to the world. Loneliness, when surrendered to God, becomes holy ground. It sharpens hearing, deepens faith, and magnifies His presence.

Encouragement for New Pastors

To any new pastor, hear this clearly: acknowledge your loneliness. Name it. Do not bury it under sermons, schedules, or smiles. It is not weakness to admit it; it is wisdom. Ministry will bring seasons when few understand the weight you carry. But you are not meant to bear it alone.

Seek out safe spaces. Where they do not exist, create them. Find mentors or trusted colleagues who will listen without judgment. These relationships save lives. Build friendships outside your congregation with people who know you as a person, not as a title. Share your struggles honestly with God, who promises never to leave or forsake you.

Guard against isolation by scheduling connections. Call friends and discuss life beyond the church. Meet with fellow pastors. Take time away with your family. Do not confuse busyness with healing; it only numbs the pain. Busyness surrounds you with people, but deepens the emptiness inside. What you need is a connection with God first, then with others who nourish your soul.

Above all, remember that you are never truly alone. The Spirit of God walks with you into every meeting, sermon, and hospital room. You may feel unseen, but you are never unattended. Your feelings are real, but God's presence is truer still. Do not deny your emotions, but do not doubt His companionship. Ministry is heavy, but it is not solitary. You walk with the One who carries you.

If you find yourself in a lonely season, take heart. Do not despair. Use it to draw closer to God, rediscover friendship, and remember that the One who called you still walks beside you.

CHAPTER 25

Cultivating Life Outside of Ministry

After I began establishing boundaries around my marriage, protecting date nights and family time, I noticed another challenge. I did not have much of a life outside of ministry. Ministry was my life. If I wasn't attending meetings, making visits, preaching sermons, or leading Bible studies, I was thinking about the church. My conversations revolved around church. My free time, when it existed, was consumed by church. I had not planned it this way, but without realizing it, I had allowed ministry to dominate every aspect of my life: my thoughts, my time, my energy, and eventually, my identity.

At first, it felt spiritual, noble, sacrificial. I told myself this was zeal, Paul-like dedication, a sign of faithfulness to God. What could possibly be wrong with giving everything to His work? Yet there is a thin line between devotion and imbalance. When ministry consumes your every thought, when it greets you in the morning and lingers at night, you are no longer serving God; you are losing yourself in a role. You stop being a person who pastors and become only the pastor. You start confusing who you are with what you do.

When your identity becomes tied entirely to ministry, your worth and purpose rise and fall with its successes and failures. Rest feels wasteful, recreation feels guilty, and joy feels undeserved. You become a ministry machine, efficient and productive, yet spiritually depleted.

This imbalance erodes not just your spirit but your humanity. It stifles your growth in all aspects: emotionally, socially, physically, and creatively. You forget the parts of yourself that once brought you life and energy. You used to laugh easily and feel deeply, but now you move through your days in muted survival mode. Ministry overshadows the person you once were. That is not God's design.

When ministry becomes your only anchor, any criticism or conflict can send you into despair. Without friendships, hobbies, or outlets beyond your role, the smallest failure can feel like a personal collapse. And when an exhausted pastor loses balance, the entire church feels it. Fatigue, irritability, and resentment ripple through the congregation. Burnout spreads quietly, but its effects are devastating.

From the beginning, God designed human beings for wholeness, not one-dimensional living. He created us to work and rest, to worship and celebrate, to lead and enjoy life. His pattern is deliberate: six days of labor and one day for renewal. The Sabbath was not a suggestion but a command. It is an invitation to joy and balance. Balance is not an interruption of ministry; it is part of the calling itself. If we fail to practice it, we have misunderstood what it means to be called.

The Lesson

Healthy pastors flourish when they cultivate a life beyond the pulpit. This does not happen by accident. It requires intention. Develop hobbies that uplift you, friendships that sustain you, and rhythms that restore you. Have people in your life who see you as a person, not only as a Pastor. Such relationships are lifelines for the soul.

Activities beyond work reconnect you with your true self. They remind you that life continues outside the church walls. For me, music has always been that outlet. Playing the saxophone frees me. It carries no deadlines, no committees, no expectations, only sound and soul. I also find peace in simple things, such as playing video games, reading non-theological books, or taking long drives. They may seem small, but they bring me back to life. They remind me that I am more than a title. I am a whole person with passions and needs, and that person deserves to be cared for.

A Biblical Reflection

Even Jesus modeled balance. After long days of healing and teaching, He often withdrew to quiet places to pray and rest, as Mark 1:35 records. He attended weddings and shared meals with friends, not only to teach but also to enjoy community. Jesus laughed, celebrated, and participated in life beyond His mission. If the Son of God required rest and fellowship, how can we claim to need less?

Ecclesiastes 3 teaches that there is a time for every purpose under heaven, which includes joy, laughter, and dancing. These are not distractions from ministry but vital expressions of divine design. The Sabbath itself reminds us that rest and joy are sacred acts of obedience. To believe that exhaustion proves dedication or that burnout reflects faithfulness is not a sign of holiness; it is a sign of pride. God does not ask of us what He did not model Himself.

Encouragement for New Pastors

If you want to last in ministry for the long haul, embrace these practices:

I. Choose one hobby that brings genuine joy. It does not have to be elaborate or expensive. It could be gardening, painting, fishing, hiking, or cooking, something that feeds your soul and reminds you that life is a gift.

II. Build friendships outside your pastoral circle. Ministry peers are valuable, but you also need people who know you as a person. These relationships allow you to be authentic and vulnerable without fear of judgment.

III. Schedule your rest. Put it on your calendar with the same seriousness as a board meeting. Protect it. Plan for it. Treat it as sacred.

IV. Reject guilt. You will feel tempted to think, "I should be visiting someone," or "I should be writing a sermon." Let that go. Rest is not rebellion; it is obedience. A rested pastor is a better shepherd.

V. Model balance for your congregation. Your members learn by watching you. When they see their pastor resting, laughing, and living joyfully, they will understand that holiness includes health. You teach them that the Sabbath is not an interruption to the mission, but the foundation of it.

Ministry never ends. There will always be another visit, another sermon, another problem. But you cannot pour from an empty cup. Hobbies and friendships are not luxuries; they are lifelines. Your spouse deserves your presence, not merely your effort. Your congregation needs your joy as much as your sermons.

Pursue joy. Laugh freely. Rest without guilt. Take time to live. Play music. Read. Travel. Dream. Do things that remind you that you are alive. Because when you live fully, you can serve faithfully.

CHAPTER 26

Protecting Your Marriage in Ministry

During my first year in ministry, I lived a considerable distance from my district, with my mother church an hour and a half away. Although I loved serving, the long commute drained my energy and spirit. By the time I returned home, I was often depleted not just physically, but emotionally and mentally. This left very little for my wife, who longed for my attention and presence.

I made countless promises about spending quality time together, whether going out to dinner or enjoying a quiet evening at home. Yet, many of those promises were broken when unexpected church matters took precedence. A meeting ran late, a member needed urgent support, or a problem arose that required my attention.

Even when I was home, my wife could tell when my mind was elsewhere. My eyes revealed it, and my words confirmed it. Our conversations about life too often drifted back to ministry. A simple question like "How was your day?" would turn into a report about church issues. The pattern was constant, frustrating, and familiar.

I told myself this was normal. Surely, every pastor struggles with balance. Wasn't this what faithfulness looked like? I justified everything with spiritual language. "It's for the Lord." "This is important." "My wife will understand." But I was wrong. I had mistaken busyness for devotion and workaholism for zeal.

Eventually, I realized I was neglecting my first calling. Before I was ever a pastor, I was a husband. That was my primary ministry, and I was failing in it. One day, my wife said half-jokingly, "Sometimes I feel like I'm your assistant or your associate pastor." Her words cut deeply. Though said lightly, they carried truth. She had become a ministry partner instead of a cherished companion. I had married a partner, not an employee, and it was time I treated her as such.

The Lesson

Your marriage is your first ministry, not your church, and it must be guarded with clear, firm, and loving boundaries. The church will demand everything you have, but you must not give it everything. Save something for home. When you give the church what rightfully belongs to your spouse and family, you are not being faithful; you are being careless with the gift God entrusted to you.

Without boundaries, passion for ministry can easily turn into neglect. Neglect breeds resentment. Resentment becomes distance. Distance leads to collapse. The pattern is slow but sure. She begins to resent the church, you begin to resent her resentment, and your marriage begins to crumble while you are busy trying to hold the church together.

Ministry is sacred, but so is marriage. It is a covenant before God, one that must never be sacrificed on the altar of church work. To place ministry above your marriage is to elevate God's mission above God's design. That is not faithfulness; it is foolishness.

A Biblical Reflection

Paul writes in Ephesians 5:25, "Husbands, love your wives just as Christ loved the church and gave himself up for her." The comparison is deliberate. Christ loved the church with sacrificial devotion, and husbands are called to love their wives with the same level of commitment and care. Notice that Paul does not say, "Love your church as Christ loved the church." That would suit many pastors, but Scripture is clear: love your wife.

This love places your wife before your career, your reputation, your ministry success, and even your congregation's expectations. When Paul lists the qualifications for spiritual leaders in 1 Timothy 3, he begins with the home. A pastor who neglects his family disqualifies himself from caring for God's household. The issue is not preaching ability but personal integrity. God values the home more than the pulpit. If your wife is lonely, your children are distant, and your home is spiritually cold, no sermon can redeem that failure.

Ministry begins at home. If you fail there, you have failed everywhere else. God never asked you to save His church by losing your family.

Encouragement for New Pastors

Protect your marriage at all costs. It is worth more than any district, appointment, or promotion. Listen to the wisdom of older pastors who have completed their race. When they look back, their deepest regrets are not missed meetings or uncompleted projects. They regret missed birthdays, forgotten anniversaries, and lost moments with their children. They say with sorrow, "I was there, but I wasn't there." That confession should be enough to sober every young pastor.

When you leave a church, your members will eventually move on. They will adapt to a new pastor, but your wife will never forget the moments when she came second. Your children will not remember your sermons, but they will remember your absence. Some will carry that pain for years, resenting not only the church but also God. No church is worth that.

So how can you protect your marriage in ministry?

I. Set boundaries. Establish non-negotiable times for your spouse and family. Have consistent date nights. Turn off your phone when you are with them. The church will survive an unanswered call.

II. Communicate clearly and publicly. Let your members know which evenings or days are reserved for your family. Guard them firmly. Say no without guilt or explanation.

III. Seek accountability. Invite your spouse to speak honestly about how you are doing with balance. Ask questions such as, "Do you feel prioritized? Do I make time for us?" Then listen without defending yourself. Adjust accordingly.

IV. Honor your spouse. Do it both privately and publicly. Let your congregation see you cherish her. When you honor her openly, you teach others to do the same in their homes.

V. Think about your legacy. When your ministry ends and the years pass, it will not be your congregation sitting beside you in old age. It will be your spouse. Invest now in the person who will walk with you long after the church doors close behind you.

I have made a pledge to my wife and daughter that I will never sacrifice them for the sake of ministry. They come first, after God and before everything else. That is my conviction and my line in the sand. I will attend the birthdays, remember the anniversaries, show up at recitals and graduations, and be present at family dinners. Whatever matters to them matters to me. My wife and daughter are not competitors with my ministry; they are my ministry.

If you take nothing else from this chapter, take this: go home, Pastor. Your family needs you. Resist the urge to be a public success and a private failure. Do not lose your family for the sake of the church. It belongs to Christ, not to you. He can sustain it without your absence from home. Protect your marriage. Your calling depends on it. Your legacy depends on it. Your soul depends on it. Go home!

PART VIII – THE TRUST TEST

CHAPTER 27

The Trust Test

Stewardship is one of humanity's most fundamental and profound responsibilities. At its core, it is about faithfully managing what God has entrusted to us. We are caretakers of what God has temporarily placed in our hands.

Stewardship encompasses every aspect of life, including our time, talents, temple, and treasures. These four areas, often referred to as the Four T's, form the foundation of how we honor God in our daily living, not only on the Sabbath.

For pastors, stewardship is not simply a subject to preach about; it must be a lifestyle to model. The principle "Do as I do, not just as I say" holds. Your life is the sermon. Your habits are the message. Your example is the altar call. Members are observant. They may never confront you, but they will imitate what they see.

If you are careless with your health, perhaps being overweight or living without discipline, you will treat your body the same way. If you are frequently late, unprepared, or disorganized, they will excuse those same traits in themselves. If you return tithes only when convenient but skip them when finances are tight, you undermine every stewardship message you preach.

Paul reminds us in 1 Corinthians 4:2, "Moreover, it is required in stewards that a man be found faithful." The divine standard is faithfulness, not brilliance, not eloquence, not charisma. Jesus teaches the same principle in Matthew 25 through the parable of the talents. The servants are not compared to one another but judged by how faithfully they used what they were given. The measure of success in stewardship is always faithfulness.

As pastors, we must remember that nothing we possess belongs to us. Not our money, not our time, not our opportunities, not even our influence. We are managers, not owners. The church belongs to God. Our role is to care for what He has entrusted to us until He returns.

Our calling is to be faithful with time, to develop the talents He has placed within us, to care for our health as His temple, and to manage our finances as His resources. This is stewardship in its truest sense. The congregation knows when a pastor lives this way. They may never say it aloud, but they notice. Your actions will always speak louder than your words.

When I began ministry, my wife and I made a deliberate commitment to live as faithful stewards in every area of life, not only in finances. We knew that our example would set the tone. We managed our time carefully, kept our word, and valued punctuality. We cared for our bodies by eating a plant-based diet and exercising regularly. We were not perfect, but we were consistent. We gave faithfully, returning tithe first and offering generously. These decisions were made not because we were being watched, but because we were accountable to God.

The results surprised us. Without any campaign, lecture, or guilt-driven sermon, members began to imitate the example. Fellowship meals changed. More members chose healthier foods and smaller portions. Giving increased. Tithes became more consistent, offerings more generous, and more people volunteered to serve. Stewardship became a culture that spread quietly through modeling, not pressure.

The Lesson

Stewardship in the church always begins with the pastor. It is not the treasurer's duty or the elders' responsibility. It starts with you. Your faithfulness sets the tone, your consistency establishes the standard, and your discipline shapes the culture.

You cannot lead others into what you refuse to practice. To preach stewardship while living without it is hypocrisy. The members will see it, resent it, and ignore your words. Stewardship is not about perfection; it is about consistency and integrity. People can overlook flaws, but they cannot ignore inconsistency or dishonesty. Faithful stewardship fosters credibility, and credibility in turn builds trust. That is leadership.

A Biblical Reflection

The first example of stewardship appears in the Garden of Eden. God, the Master, entrusted Adam with His creation. Adam owned nothing. Everything belonged to God. His task was to care for the garden, cultivating and protecting it. His role was to manage what was God's, under God's authority, in accordance with God's will.

When Adam failed in that responsibility, the consequences extended far beyond himself. A failure in stewardship never affects only the steward; it also impacts those who are being stewarded. The same is true for pastors today. When we fail to be faithful managers, the effects ripple through the congregation.

Paul captures this truth again in 1 Corinthians 4:2: "Moreover, it is required in stewards that a man be found faithful." Faithfulness, not success, remains the divine measure. In the parable of the talents, the Master praises servants not for the size of their return, but for their faithfulness with what they had.

Encouragement for New Pastors

Be a steward before you are a preacher. Your ministry will be judged not by your sermons alone, but by your stewardship. How you handle your body, time, gifts, and money will either build or weaken your influence.

Here are a few practical steps:

> **I. Return your tithe faithfully.** Always give God the first portion. Do not expect from your members what you do not do yourself. Faithfulness with little proves readiness for more.

> **II. Practice integrity with church funds.** Every dollar in the church belongs to God. Manage it transparently. Keep records. Avoid even the appearance of impropriety. Personal needs must never be met with church money.

III. Be disciplined with time. Show respect for others by showing up on time. Keep appointments. Work hard, but rest regularly. God established a rhythm of six days for labor and one day for renewal. Follow it.

IV. Care for your health. Your body is the temple of the Holy Spirit. A pastor who is sick or exhausted cannot serve effectively. Eat well, rest enough, and schedule medical checkups. Remember, dead pastors do not preach.

V. Teach stewardship holistically. Do not limit it to finances. Teach your members to be faithful with time, talent, temple, and treasure. Stewardship is not a segment of Christian life; it is the sum of it.

Stewardship is one of the most visible tests of a pastor's credibility. Conferences measure it in reports, and congregations measure it in example. Churches with growing faithfulness and generosity often have pastors who model both. When you are consistent in stewardship, you not only honor God but also inspire others to do the same.

Be faithful. Be consistent. Lead by example, and watch transformation begin through you.

PART IX – MINISTRY BEYOND THE WALLS

CHAPTER 28

Pastor Your Community

When I arrived in Mississippi, I was struck by how deeply the community respected pastors. I did not expect that. Coming from the Northeast, where religious authority is often questioned or dismissed, the South felt entirely different. In an era when scandals and hypocrisy have eroded public trust in spiritual leaders, I discovered in the Deep South, especially in Mississippi, part of what many refer to as the Bible Belt, that pastors are still held in high regard.

I remember walking into a convenience store one afternoon and seeing a group of young men laughing and joking outside. The moment they realized I was a pastor, they immediately put out their cigarettes. "Sorry, Pastor, didn't see you there," one said.

Another time, I passed by a house where several men were drinking outside. As soon as they noticed me, they hid their bottles behind their chairs. "We respect you, Pastor," they said. They did not say they respected God or the church, but me. That moment taught me that in this culture, the title "Pastor" carries real personal weight.

The same thing happened when I overheard people using profanity. Their tone changed as soon as they saw me. "Oh, sorry, Pastor," they said without me having to say a word. I had not demanded respect; it was offered to me. What surprised me most was that many of these individuals were not members of my church. Some had never even attended any church, yet they showed a natural respect for the pastoral office.

In the South, pastors matter even to those who are not churchgoers. Ironically, I often felt more honored by the community than by my own members. A grocery clerk would call me "Pastor" with warmth, while some members said the same title with suspicion or critique. Strangers respected me, but church members sometimes resisted me. That contrast stung.

Church members often view their pastor through the lens of structure and tradition. They see you in the boardroom making decisions, in the pulpit preaching sermons they analyze, or at committee meetings discussing budgets they question. Their respect often depends on how well you meet their expectations, which are shaped by habit, culture, and personality.

The community, however, carries no such expectations. They are not interested in church politics or policies. They do not care who was elected to a particular position or what the church manual states. They see pastors in simpler terms as moral voices, prayer partners, and people who bring comfort and wisdom.

Still, not everyone in the community is impressed by the title. For some, "Pastor" is just another job description. It earns no respect until you prove trustworthy. These are the people for whom your presence matters most. You begin with no credibility, and you build it only by showing up, listening, and serving. Trust grows slowly, but it grows surely.

The Lesson

You do not pastor only your church. You also pastor your community. Ministry was never meant to be confined to four walls. Every person in your city, the store clerk, the barber, the school coach, the mayor, is part of your pastoral field. Once you see them as part of your calling, ministry expands beyond attendance and offerings into actual influence.

The community values authenticity more than titles. They care less about your theology and more about your presence. They will not remember your denominational statements, but they will remember that you stood beside them after a fire, prayed with them at a hospital, or showed up after a storm. While the church measures your sermons, the community measures your compassion. Both are vital.

A Biblical Reflection

Jesus modeled this balance perfectly. Matthew 4:23 says He went throughout all Galilee, teaching in the synagogues and healing the sick. He met spiritual and physical needs together. People loved Him because He met them where they were. Yet, when He returned to His hometown, Nazareth, the same people who had grown up with Him dismissed Him. "Is this not the carpenter's son?" they asked. Among strangers, He was honored; among the familiar, He was rejected.

Paul experienced the same tension. In Berea, people received him eagerly, studying his words. In Lystra, they beat and stoned him. The same preacher, the same gospel, met both reverence and rejection. Respect and resistance can coexist in ministry.

Encouragement for New Pastors

For new pastors, this dual experience is both humbling and freeing. You cannot control how people respond to you, and you are not responsible for it. Some will love you, others will dismiss you, but faithfulness is your focus. Church approval and community respect are blessings, not requirements. God's approval is what ultimately matters.

Here are some practical ways to live this out:

I. Be visible in your community. Attend civic events, school meetings, and town gatherings. Let people see you outside of the pulpit. Be present, approachable, and known.

II. Show up during crises. When tragedy strikes, be there: a fire, a shooting, or a flood. You do not need a sermon; your presence will preach for you.

III. Respect both perspectives. Acknowledge that the church and the community see you differently. One measures structure, the other measures sincerity. Both views deserve attention and grace.

IV. Redefine your role. Help your congregation understand that serving the community strengthens the church. When the community respects the pastor, the church's witness expands.

You are not called to choose between pastoring the church and pastoring the community. You are called to do both. The church may pay your salary, but the community tests your influence. Both matter to God.

Pastor your church faithfully, but do not neglect the world beyond it. Sometimes, the stranger who respects you on the street opens a door the church never could. That door may lead to new partnerships, gospel opportunities, or civic influence that advances the kingdom of God.

Community respect creates kingdom access. Cherish it, nurture it, and use it for God's glory. Be more than a church pastor. Be a community pastor.

CHAPTER 29

Your Vision Is Limited; Rely on the Holy Spirit

One of the humbling realities of ministry is that, no matter how much you plan, the limits of your vision will always show. You can only see so far. You can anticipate some variables, but not all of them. Even your best planning cannot foresee everything. When you believe you have a solid plan and that every detail has been considered, life and ministry will remind you that human perspective is narrow compared to God's infinite wisdom. He sees what you cannot: past, present, and future, and His purposes reach beyond imagination.

Early in my pastoral journey, I leaned heavily on logic and structure, adopting an MBA mindset and business strategies. I believed that if I worked hard enough, putting in sixty-hour workweeks and crafting detailed strategic plans, everything would fall into place. I was wrong. Ministry belongs to God. It is His work, His people, and His kingdom. Every decision, direction, and detail must be guided by His Spirit, not by human logic.

I recall one evangelistic series that seemed perfect on paper. We had professional flyers, a clear budget, organized transportation, a shuttle schedule, music teams, and a complete menu plan. It looked flawless. Yet, when opening night arrived, attendance was half of what we had expected, and the volunteers were inconsistent. Some came one night but not the next. The energy was low, and I grew discouraged. This was not what I had planned.

Only when I surrendered the series completely to prayer did things change. Once I released control and followed the Spirit's leading instead of my plans, transformation happened. People responded, hearts opened, and baptisms followed not because of my planning, but despite it.

This lesson deepened during the evangelistic series in Tunica. It was a small town with few resources. We had done all the groundwork, but no amount of planning could have guaranteed the results. The Spirit moved in ways beyond my design. People appeared who were never on our lists, had never been contacted, and had never been invited. They came, responded to altar calls, and surrendered their lives to Christ. By the end of the series, twenty people had been baptized. Some said, "I watched online," or "My friend told me." None of it was my doing. It was entirely the Spirit's work.

The Lesson

Pastors must not depend solely on vision casting, strategic plans, or leadership models. These can serve a purpose, but without the Spirit's presence, they become human ambition disguised in religious language. Human vision is limited by time, experience, and personal perspective. The Spirit's vision is eternal and continuously aligned with God's will.

When we lead only by our own insight, we risk guiding people according to our plans rather than God's. That is the danger: creating followers of ourselves instead of followers of Christ.

True leadership in ministry begins with surrender. Learn to pause, pray, and wait for direction. Trust the Spirit's timing. Allow Him to interrupt, delay, or redirect your plans. His wisdom is never wrong, and His pace is always perfect.

A Biblical Reflection

Scripture continually reminds us of the boundaries of human vision. Proverbs 16:9 declares, "In their hearts humans plan their course, but the Lord establishes their steps." We plan, but God determines. The order matters: we plan, He directs. James echoes this truth when he warns against presuming on tomorrow, reminding us that our lives are like a mist, temporary, fragile, and fleeting. God's plans, however, are eternal.

In Acts 16, Paul planned to preach in Asia and Bithynia. His strategy was logical and sound, but the Holy Spirit prevented him. Instead, through a vision, God sent him to Macedonia. That redirection opened doors to Lydia's conversion, the salvation of the Philippian jailer, and the founding of the Philippian church. Had Paul insisted on his own plan, he would have missed God's larger purpose. Even good plans can hinder God's best plans when the Spirit does not lead them.

Jesus taught the same principle. In John 16:13, He promised His disciples that the Spirit would guide them into all truth. The keyword is "guide." Guidance implies movement, dependence, and trust. Their success would come not from strategy, but from surrender to divine direction.

Encouragement for New Pastors

So what do you do when God disrupts your plans? Hold every vision lightly. Planning tools, vision boards, and strategies are helpful, but they must remain subject to the Spirit's authority. Pray over every plan and ask God to interrupt when it doesn't align with His will. Let Him cancel meetings, shift priorities, and reorder schedules.

Cultivate the discipline of spiritual listening. Set aside quiet moments away from the noise of ministry. Fast, pray, and invite trusted mentors to help you discern God's voice. Their prayers and counsel can protect you from unwise choices.

When the Spirit redirects you, especially when His direction seems illogical, trust Him. His view is wider than yours. Ministry success will never come from human cleverness but from obedience to the Spirit.

Wait, when He says "not yet." Move when He says "go." Rest when He says "wait." His voice always leads to fruit that lasts. Your plans may fail without His power, but His plans never fail. Stop trusting your vision and start trusting His Spirit. That is where wisdom begins. That is where faithful ministry begins.

PART X – BROKEN YET BECOMING

CHAPTER 30

If Anything Else Brings You Joy, Do That

I have experienced many moments when ministry felt like it was breaking me. The criticism was sharp, the exhaustion constant, the loneliness heavy, and the disappointment crushing. During those times, I became harsh with myself and began to believe I was failing not only in ministry but in life itself. Spiritually, I felt distant from God.

There were evenings when I left board meetings completely defeated, watching my carefully laid plans unravel before me. Proposals were rejected, ideas dismissed, and visions questioned. Some members openly opposed me, spreading lies or withdrawing their support when I needed it most. I saw my best sermons fall flat. I poured months of preparation into evangelistic campaigns that yielded little fruit, far from what I had prayed for or imagined.

In those seasons, questions lingered: Why am I doing this? Why did I sign up for this?

These are the moments that reveal the fine print of ministry. You sign up to preach, baptize, celebrate victories, and serve God with joy. Hidden within that same calling, however, are sleepless nights, deep discouragement, and the pain of leading people who sometimes do not want to be led.

The Lesson

Breaking occurs when we try to engage in divine work while still being human. The ministry places us in the midst of a real war, a spiritual conflict with a relentless enemy who shows no mercy. The struggle is both external and internal, battles with pride, insecurity, fear, and doubt. It stretches every part of who you are.

Dry seasons last longer than expected. Marriages are tested. Resources seem insufficient. At times, you whisper to yourself, "This is not what I signed up for." Yet here lies the beautiful paradox of ministry: when it breaks you, God remakes you. The breaking is the remaking. The breaking strips away pride and illusion, forcing you into total dependence on Him. Through pain, you discover what grace truly means.

A Biblical Reflection

Jeremiah knew that breaking point well. Tired and defeated, he resolved to quit. Yet he later confessed, "His word is in my heart like a fire, a fire shut up in my bones; I am weary of holding it in, indeed I cannot" (Jeremiah 20:9). Even when Jeremiah wanted to stop, God would not let him.

Elijah felt the same despair, collapsing under a broom tree and pleading for death. Yet God restored him not through thunder or flame, but through a gentle whisper. He gave him food, rest, and reassurance (1 Kings 19:4–12). God meets His broken prophets not with judgment, but with tenderness.

Paul too testified from experience: "My grace is sufficient for you, for My power is made perfect in weakness" (2 Corinthians 12:9). Weakness is not failure; it is the soil where grace grows. God allows His servants to be broken, not to destroy them but to reshape them. Breaking is the crucible of ministry, and remaking is the grace that sustains it.

Encouragement for New Pastors

If God has not called you to this work, walk away without guilt. Ministry is not for everyone, and there is no shame in discerning that. If your motivation is driven by family expectations, status, or security, step back and seek your true calling. God has one for you, but it may not be this.

However, if you are convinced that God has called you, then settle this truth in your heart: you will be broken repeatedly. Yet in every breaking, God will rebuild you stronger. The board meetings that drain you will drive you deeper into prayer. The sermons that fall flat will refine your study. Betrayals will remind you that Jesus, too, was betrayed. Failures will humble you and anchor you in grace. Through each trial, you will learn that ministry cannot be done in your own strength; it requires grace that sustains, empowers, and transforms.

At the same time, remember that the ministry's rewards outweigh its pain. The joy of witnessing a soul rise from the waters of baptism, the comfort of praying with grieving families, and the fulfillment of watching young people discover their purpose - these moments remind us why we endure, why we stay, and why we persevere.

Ministry is not ultimately about preaching or administration; it is about a relentless God who works through our brokenness to redeem us. Your salvation is part of that process. God is not only using you to reach others; He is using ministry to reach you. The greater the breaking, the greater the remaking. That is the mystery and the beauty of God's call.

EPILOGUE

The Journey Continues

When I began writing these reflections late at night at my desk, I never intended to produce a manual with formulas for pastoral success or a list of guaranteed steps to church growth. Ministry does not operate that way. It never has and never will. It is unpredictable, complex, and deeply human. Each congregation carries its own rhythm, its own wounds, and its own measure of grace. Yet, amid all that unpredictability, God's fingerprints are everywhere, quietly shaping the work in ways no method ever could.

What I have written here is not theory; it is testimony. These lessons have been carved into my soul through tears, late-night prayers, public failures, small victories, unexpected baptisms, and quiet moments of grace. These words are written with scars, not ink.

If there is one truth that ties all these reflections together, it is this: ministry is not about what you accomplish for God but about what God accomplishes in you through ministry. It is the crucible where sanctification happens. God is far more interested in transforming you than in merely using you. He wants your heart more than your hands.

Every board meeting, even the difficult ones; every baptism, even when the number is small; every dry season; every criticism; and every fleeting joy, all are part of God's sanctifying work. Nothing is wasted: not the pain, not the disappointment, and not even the betrayal. You will be broken, but you will also be remade. Therefore, keep walking, even if you limp. Keep preaching, even if your voice trembles. Keep serving, even when you feel empty. Above all, remain in Christ. Stay connected to the Vine, because apart from Him, ministry loses its power and becomes noise.

A Charge to the New Pastor

None of us has it all together. Yet God delights in using what is broken. You will stumble and question yourself. You will wrestle with doubt and fatigue. You will wonder whether you are enough. But in those moments, you will also witness miracles, small, quiet miracles that remind you that His grace is always sufficient. For every season. Every task. Every impossibility.

Do not measure your ministry by comparison; it will only poison your soul. Do not let failure or fear silence your calling. They do not disqualify you; they refine you. And never forget this truth: before the title, before the degree, before the ordination, you are first and always a child of God. That identity is what sustains you when everything else fades.

Preach Christ, not yourself. Love people, even the difficult ones. Protect your family; they are your first congregation. Be faithful to your spouse, your calling, and your God. Keep showing up. God does not demand perfection; He asks for faithfulness.

The flock is not yours; it never was. It belongs to the Chief Shepherd. You are His under-shepherd, called to lead with humility and to follow with courage. Follow Him. That is the charge. That is the call. That is pastoral ministry in its truest form.

The Preacher's Prayer

Lord,

Thank you for calling us into this sacred work. We confess that the weight of ministry is often more than we can bear. We have been discouraged, lonely, and at times even ready to quit. But in those very moments, You have reminded us that Your strength is made perfect in our weakness.

Teach us to serve faithfully, not for recognition but for Your glory. Teach us to rest, not in our own efforts but in Your promises. Protect our families, guard our hearts, and renew our spirits when we are weary.

May every sermon we preach, every soul we reach, and every act of service we render point people back to You. And when ministry breaks us, remake us in Your image so that we reflect the grace of Christ to all who look on.

We ask for courage to endure, wisdom to lead, and humility to follow wherever You guide. Keep us faithful until the day we see You face to face.

In Jesus' name, Amen.

www.ingramcontent.com/pod-product-compliance
Lightning Source LLC
Chambersburg PA
CBHW071200160426
43196CB00011B/2136